The Lord's Harvest
and the
Rural Church

The Lord's Harvest and the Rural Church

A New Look at Ministry in the Agri-Culture

KENT R. HUNTER

Beacon Hill Press of Kansas City
Kansas City, Missouri

10   9   8   7   6   5   4   3   2   1

This book is dedicated to
the people of Zion Lutheran Church,
Corunna, Ind.

Other Books by Kent R. Hunter:

Courageous Churches
(with Paul Heinecke and David Luecke)

Facing the Facts for Church Growth
(with Diane Barber)

Foundations for Church Growth

Gifted for Growth

Launching Growth in the Local Congregation

Moving the Church into Action

The Road to Church Growth

Six Faces of the Christian Church

Your Church Has Doors

Your Church Has Personality

Contents

Foreword

The rural church has been one of the most important social institutions throughout American history. And yet, very little is known about it. Denominational leaders know how important their rural churches are. Lay leaders in rural churches know. However, they haven't had much help in understanding what makes their church tick and how churches like theirs can be improved.

Kent Hunter will be a lifelong friend to all who love and appreciate the rural church. This book will take its place alongside *Burpee's Seed Catalog, The Farm Journal,* the operator's manual for the new baler, and the newsletter from the county extension agent. It is just as practical and useful as any of the above. I say "lifelong friend" because Kent Hunter is so positive and upbeat about the rural church that readers will feel his kindred spirit immediately. And rural friendships are known to be long lasting.

Kent comes with expertise on the growth of churches equivalent to the expertise of the local veterinarian on the health of cows. It was as late as the mid-1970s when the Church Growth Movement began to take root in American soil, having flourished previously on the mission field. Kent Hunter was one of the pioneers in those early days, receiving his doctorate in the field. His many books and instructional manuals and his strategic Church Growth Center, along with his enviable track record as a researcher and consultant, have secured him a place in the top echelon of church growth leaders. He was recently honored by being elected president of the North American Society of Church Growth, and he succeeds Donald McGavran, the founder of the

Church Growth Movement, as editor of the prestigious *Global Church Growth* magazine.

Hunter's treatment of the rural church is not limited to families that have balers and run cattle. It is much broader. Rural churches to him include: cornfield churches, county seat churches, small-town churches, solo churches, playground churches, shrinking churches, metro-satellite churches, suburban fringe churches, migrant churches, and even nonchurch churches. What a spectrum! But he skillfully highlights characteristics that such churches have in common and provides valuable suggestions to leaders as to how to deal with them.

Since I am a farmer by background myself, I was especially impressed that Kent knew what he was talking about when I read his principle of "the miracle of the corncob" and his straight advice to "treat your money like manure." He talks our language. He probes the psychology of rural churches and analyzes their health and vitality better than any other I have seen. But he also goes on to spell out solutions to many of the problems rural churches have. Few books have more practical advice on how to reap the Lord's harvest in your community. It even has solid hints on how to handle finances.

I greatly appreciate the fact that Kent Hunter is growth oriented, but he is not growth obsessed. If this book helps your church grow, we will rejoice and I believe the angels in heaven will rejoice. If it doesn't, you will understand the reasons why and still rest assured that your church is part of the beautiful bride of Christ and you will be together with Him at the marriage feast!

C. PETER WAGNER
Fuller Theological Seminary
Pasadena, Calif.

Acknowledgments

As with any significant research project, there are many people behind the scenes who work tirelessly to support those who write materials like this book.

I am grateful to the people of Zion Lutheran Church: a feisty, warm, loving, challenging group—some from agriculture and some not—that God brought together during several very exciting and joyful years of ministry. I am thankful to Cathy Eshelman for her efficient style as church secretary.

I am grateful also to the Church Growth Center staff who helped with various aspects of this manuscript: Geraldine Dettmann, Kathy Buss, and Jody Ford. I also thank Rebecca Gates, Royal Natzke, and Peggy Baldwin. I appreciate Alan Barber for his insights and Tony Steinbronn for his critique.

Finally, God has blessed me with a wonderful wife, Janet, whose constant encouragement is a vital ingredient of support. Together with our children, Laura and Jonathan, we continue to celebrate our life on the farm, dabble in agriculture, and I consult with churches of all sizes and types in many places around the world. I am grateful to God for the best of both worlds!

1

What Is Rural?

"Joe, are you a member of that church on the edge of Harpersville?" asked Bill. Every month for 10 years Bill had come into Joe's barbershop. He could always count on getting a good haircut and receiving an update on all the town gossip. Somehow, though, over the 10 years the two had never talked about church.

"Sure, I go there," replied Joe. "My wife grew up in that church, and when we were married I joined it."

"It's a little rural church, isn't it, Joe?" asked Bill.

Joe thought a minute. It was a small, white frame building on the edge of the little town. To the north it was all countryside. It was a picturesque little church, nestled between rolling hills that were so common to that area. It had been built over 150 years ago by early settlers who had come to farm. As mechanization entered the scene, the "little farmers" sold out. Those that stayed with it continued to acquire more and more land. Now only a few church members were farmers, and these farmers worked like executives of small corporations. Most of the other people in the church worked in town. Some drove from the city 30 miles east.

"Well?" Bill interrupted Joe's thoughts.

"Yes, I guess you could call it rural," said Joe. "It's a real friendly country church."

The face of the rural church has been changing. Joe wasn't sure what to call his church. It certainly had been rural at one time. It seemed to have some characteristics of rural life. Yet the members' life-styles, occupations, and perspectives on the world were radically different from those of their predecessors 100 years ago. Joe was confused. Just what does it mean to be a rural church? he wondered.

There are many studies and stories about the rural church, but very few of them define what they mean by *rural*. Most of the literature leaves people in a fog of uncertainty. This fog has clouded the value of research that could help the church become more effective in its mission and programming.

The Small Church in the Country

While the rural church is rarely defined, it is usually implied that it is a church in a sparsely populated area, and it is often referred to as being small. These two characteristics are so vague that diagnostic studies are difficult to conduct. Comparisons among churches become confusing because some churches that are designated rural are not small by any standards, and some so-called rural churches are not in the country. Some are little white frame buildings, and some are not.

The designation of *rural* in much of the literature comes from the definition given by the United States Census Bureau. Depending on who is determining the particular size, a rural place will be defined as being a nonmetropolitan area where less than a certain number of people live. Or rural churches could be described as churches located in a community of 2,500 or less population which have an average attendance of 25 to 100 people in worship on Sunday mornings. These churches are placed together in the category of rural and compared as though they are the same kind of church.

Churches classified as rural in the traditional way are not necessarily alike. Viewing them so not only is inaccurate but also can lead to stereotypes that are detrimental for planning, program development, the creation of resources by the denomination, and the training of professional church workers.

Take the Community Christian Church at Westpoint. Westpoint was a sleepy little town 27 miles from a major metropolitan area. Nine years ago one of the major landowners sold his farm to a development corporation that then built hundreds of suburban-type apartment complexes. Since there was a shortage of this type of housing in the city, many people moved to Westpoint and commuted to work. A drugstore was built, then a fastfood restaurant, several banks, and a small shopping plaza. Westpoint's population jumped from 200 to 2,000 in a short time. Davenport is still farther out from the city. Many people who live in Davenport shop in Westpoint on their way home from work. Is Westpoint a rural town?

Before the apartment boom, the town had only one small church, whose minister served that church and four others in the country. This community church is now a growing church in a bedroom community of a large metropolitan city. Is it a rural church? According to traditional definition, it is. Yet, how can it be compared to Mount Zion Church just 10 miles northeast of Westpoint, which has a membership of dairy farmers scattered throughout the countryside?

The problem of definition works the other way as well. What about Holy Ghost Church in Centerville with a membership of 880? Worship attendance is 450 on a good Sunday. Attendance is lowest when the men are in the fields in the spring and at harvesttime in the autumn. Everyone knows everyone. Most of them are related to each other. It's one big, happy family. If you walk through the cemetery behind the church, you can follow the history of many of the larger families whose great-grandchildren now operate the family farms—and the church—still today. Yet, by definition, this may not be called a rural church.

The problem of the definition of *rural* also has repercussions for urban churches. Strictly speaking, a community of 2,500 or less is very common in pluralistic urban areas. This is especially clear to the biblically minded Christian who sees the world the way God sees it—as a mosaic of people groups. These people groups are communities. The Census Bureau ignores this fact, but the church cannot. Consequently, there are hundreds of urban churches with under 150 worshipers on Sunday morning whose members belong to a Hispanic, Black, Chinese, or Italian community. To classify them as rural would be useless.

The confusion over the definition of the term *rural* has

caused many people to abandon it. Most church consultants have found that classifying churches by size is much more useful for diagnosing ills and prescribing improvements for Christian congregations. There are many good reasons for categorizing churches by size. Churches of similar size are often the same in organizational structure, programming needs, and challenges. The small church is a kind of organism different from the medium-sized or large church. Small churches behave like other small churches. Medium-sized churches are very similar to other medium-sized churches. Large churches share many characteristics with other large churches.

Should the use of the term *rural* be discarded entirely? Does it serve any purpose for diagnosing the health and growth of certain churches? The answer comes as we redefine the term and begin to remove the fog of confusion. It is an important task because for the first time in decades, many countries in the world are beginning to see a reversal of the urban in-migration and metropolitan sprawl. In spite of the high cost of energy and the transportation congestion, many people are jumping over the suburbs to the outlying areas. In the United States, the great escape from the labor unions is causing many factories to move from northern, urban areas to small towns where labor is less expensive. As this out-migration continues, people will be joining all kinds of churches "out there" in the country. Some of these people will be joining what we will redefine as rural churches.

Redefining *Rural*

The dictionary describes *rural* in basically three ways: open country, rustic, agriculturally oriented. The first definition is the traditional way of describing a rural church. A better definition is: *A rural church is a congregation of Christian people who live an agriculturally oriented life-style.* It is a church made up of a people group who belong to the agricultural community.

Rural is a mind-set. It is a way of life. It is not poor or rich; not necessarily educated or uneducated. It is not necessarily better or worse than other life-styles. But the rural orientation to life carries with it characteristics that have an enormous impact on a

Christian church. It helps describe not only *what* people think but also *how* they think—how they perceive reality. It helps to describe how they perceive their church.

As mechanization leads to larger and larger farms, the world has less and less people who are genuinely rural, as it has been redefined here. Whereas 90 percent of the people in the United States produced 100 percent of the food 100 years ago, now only 2 or 3 percent of the people produce 120 percent of the food. A smaller number of people are producing at least 20 percent more food than is needed. As the number of agricultural workers gets smaller, the number of rural churches will decline. As nonagricultural people fill rural churches and become a significant majority, a transformational change occurs. The church becomes a different kind of organism.

Recognizing the unique perspectives of a rural, agricultural worldview is the beginning of developing effective ways to do ministry in rural areas. In changing areas, it is a way to recognize and deal with tensions that arise. It is a way of acknowledging the genuine and beautiful uniqueness of churches that are truly rural. Understanding these characteristics enables pastors to serve more effectively and congregations to plan and work toward health and growth, as the Lord gives the increase.

2

The Personality of the Rural Church

*T*he rural church can be redefined to include only those chur ˈes where the majority of the members are involved in agricultural work. Their orientation to life sets them apart as a homogeneous unit of people. Their common ground is not determined by where they live, how dense the population of the area, or by the size of the church to which they belong. Their commonality is a view of life that runs in their blood. It is beautiful; it is unique.

A Unique Organism

Like any homogeneous group, rural people have common characteristics. These characteristics are not totally unique to rural people. There is overlap. Some of these characteristics can be found in people who are not rural now but who are second-generation rural people. These characteristics may fade if their children and grandchildren continue down a nonrural path. Then there are those nonrural people who live in an area where most of their neighbors and friends are rural. Some of these people will melt, to some degree, as they are influenced by the surrounding attitudes and life-styles. In spite of these exceptions, there is still a significant homogeneity enabling us to define rural people by certain characteristics. When the rural church is seen as a unique organism, the potential to develop effective strategies for growth will increase.

Strategies That Fit

Jesus Christ is Lord of the harvest. Only He can build the

Church, but He calls laborers to work in His harvest. People enter the picture of God's great design to make disciples of all peoples. Strategy is essential. A wheat field may be ripe for harvest. God brought the increase, but it takes people to do the harvesting. A corn picker will not do the job. There is one machine that works best. Why? Because of the uniqueness of wheat. This is also true of the strategies for mission and ministry in the rural church.

What strategies are most useful for helping a person mature in Christ? How can a church be structured to see that the members grow together in fellowship? What can be done to maximize the congregation's potential for outreach to its community? What is the best strategy for helping the local church toward planting other churches and extending its ministry to other places?

The answers to strategy questions always begin with discerning the uniqueness of each individual congregation. The local body of Christ has a personality. If that personality is based on a rural orientation, there are particular characteristics that comprise a unique set of strengths and challenges. For ministry that develops growth patterns in the rural church, it is essential to be sensitive toward those characteristics and to develop programming with them in mind.

Common Characteristics

1. *Close-knit family units.* The family units of many rural people are strong and closely knit. This is true not only of the nuclear family but of extended families as well. Generations of sons and daughters may defy the trends of a mobile society and remain in the same community—and the same church. "It seems like everyone around here is related!" reflected a newcomer at Hillside Chapel. The perception is true of many churches, but it is an especially strong characteristic of the rural church.

In a society where families are being torn apart, a church with strong family units has its strengths. There is a whole family system of checks and balances for the encouragement of worship attendance. Sunday morning is much more than a spiritual event. It is a Sabbath reunion for families. The extended family ties weld the congregation together in relationships in Christ. For children born into these families, assimilation into the church is simply an extension of other family developments. Mutual care and support is easier in a congregation of close-knit extended families because it comes naturally.

What are some of the problems that arise from close-knit families in the church? The extended family encouragement system for worship attendance works just the opposite for those who do not share that priority. For example, the Zunkel family seems more interested in making money than in attending church. It's been that way for years. Farming is their whole life. They enjoy getting together, but church falls low on the priority list. Like a contagious disease, their apathy toward the church has spread through the whole family. They even reinforce delinquency from church sometimes by planning family gatherings that conflict with church activities. A step toward reversing the situation is to determine who are the leaders of the Zunkel tribe. Each family has its tribal chief, its patriarchs or matriarchs. These are the people who often are the opinion makers. Helping that extended family get back to church regularly will probably require a change of attitude among the leaders.

While every Sunday morning is a family reunion for the church with strong family units, what about the outsider? What about the first-time visitor? What about the new person who shows up for church looking for love, acceptance, and ultimately, Jesus Christ?

To the insider, the groups that form in close circles on Sunday morning represent good communication among families and close friends. To the outsider, those circles of people standing around after church appear to be not-so-holy huddles. Backs are turned to the outside, and the visitor bounces from one closed group to another. Unless caught by a friendly opening, the outsider will bounce right out the door—perhaps never to return.

By far the best way to get visitors into the Sunday morning huddles is not to invite them but to bring them. Then they are attached to an inside person from the outset. An attitude of outreach will help people be on the lookout for the visitor who was not brought to church but who just drops in on Sunday morning.

The rural church that takes the Great Commission seriously will develop an intentional system for assimilating new Christians. (In my book *Your Church Has Doors: How to Open the Front and Close the Back*, I have developed such a system.) It is especially important for inside families to adopt new outside families who are attracted to their church.

The support system that comes naturally along *family* lines in the rural church must become a *congregational* function if the church wants to attract and keep new members. Care and support for those who are ill, shut-in, or have other needs must become both public and formal, rather than the private family lines of communication. When a family member goes to the hospital, the pastor should be notified. It should be announced in church and written in the Sunday bulletin. Public prayers should be part of the worship service. In addition to the unorganized method of cards, visits, and help from family and close friends, a formal system of caring can be established. The women's group can have a card committee. The elders can be trained to make calls that supplement the pastor's visits. These strategies take the best of the *close*-knit system in the rural church and open it so that it isn't a *closed* system to outsiders.

2. *A strong camaraderie among insiders.* The rural community is like an extended family in many ways. Since families are tied to the land for generations, the community around the rural church is not as mobile as most of modern society. This stability provides for long-term relationships. It also allows the church to develop long-range strategies. This is a strength to the church that is willing to plan ahead.

The longevity of community citizenship means that local people know each other. Evangelism and outreach should be developed along the lines of natural relationship webs—the friends and relatives of the members. A good strategy for growth simply begins by helping members identify their unchurched friends and relatives in the community. Once these are identified, members can be helped to develop a specific strategy for reaching each person. This is a real asset to the church located in a context of strong community camaraderie.

Social ministry comes naturally and spontaneously in a rural community. When the Swaggers came home one evening last winter to find their house engulfed in flames, it took only hours for the whole community to know about it. Offers were made for temporary housing. The crops were in and the weather was poor, so the men could easily find time to help the Swaggers rebuild. As soon as the outside walls were up and the building was closed from the weather, the community came forward with furniture—old and new, loaned or freely given. This experience of love and concern is not a duty. It is a way of life among rural people.

One of the greatest challenges where long-term relationships exist is that Christians can take for granted that certain people don't go to church. "I've known Harold for years," said Norman. "He hasn't gone to church since before he was married." Consequently, no one has shared the gospel with Harold for years. Some of the church members serve on the local Volunteer Fire Department with him, and they meet at least once a month—they've done it for years. But it has never occurred to them that they could be God's channel for sharing the Good News.

It is important to train God's people to share the gospel. A sophisticated, detailed, greatly structured system of evangelism may not be necessary in a rural community. Perhaps the best system would be to (a) sensitize people to evangelistic opportunities, and (b) train them to tell what Christ and the church mean to them in a natural, personal way. Witnessing may happen best at the feed mill, the barbershop, and the grocery store. In a rural church sensitized to the opportunities, it may happen as two drivers in pickups head toward each other on a country road and stop for a five-minute chat about their sows, their cotton, or Christ.

The longevity of the rural mind-set is a real plus for community relationships *if you are an insider.* The newcomer to town cannot become an insider. To some extent, this is impossible to change—especially where newcomers are significantly in the minority. Yet this provides the Christian church a great opportunity to be the community God has called it to be. The rural church is

a community within the community. The credentials for acceptance do not include lifelong membership. The credentials are
freely given through the forgiveness of Jesus Christ. The rural
church that wants to reach newcomers must focus on its great
opportunity to be an accepting community to newcomers.

Bob and Christen moved into Waynesville hoping to start a
new life for themselves. Bob had been in trouble with the law
and needed a fresh start. They tried every church in town but felt
like outsiders. They quit going to church for a while, but then
someone told them about the friendly church at Hyde's Corner.

One Sunday they made the trip out there. They experienced
acceptance and community. They were not rural people and were
not members of that denomination, but they were accepted.
They gladly travel the 30 miles to every church function. Bob
and Christen are insiders today because the people at Hyde's
Corner have a Great Commission heart.

The rural church that cares about the total welfare of people
will be sensitive to the felt needs of people in the community.
The rural church that wants to grow will train people to see opportunities to demonstrate the love of Jesus Christ. It will help
the members see needs as channels through which they can ver-
balize that salvation is by grace through faith in Jesus Christ. The
growing rural church will be like the New Testament church,
where people went everywhere proclaiming the gospel.

3. *Communication is good.* In an urban context many people
don't know the last name of the person who lives next door.
They seldom communicate. One of the great blessings of the rural community is that communication happens freely. Based on
the two factors of close-knit, extended families and a community
of camaraderie, the rural community has a context for good communication.

Since communication runs so freely, the rural church has
several advantages. When a need arises, the word gets out quickly. When Don Perkins' cattle got out, it wasn't long before everyone found out and was on the lookout for a stray steer.

One of the best ways to encourage church growth is to reinforce a positive attitude among the people of the church. One

way is to capitalize on victories. The informal network system of communication in the rural church is an excellent forum through which this can happen. For example, one pastor looked at his denominational statistics and discovered 15 churches in his region that were of similar size. His congregation ranked eighth, so 7 were a little larger and 7 were slightly smaller. Then he ranked his church from the standpoint of those who were unchurched joining the church—conversion growth. It ranked first. He ranked the church on the basis of Sunday School attendance. It ranked third. He checked it in the area of per capita giving, and it ranked second. Instead of making a formal announcement in church about this, this pastor recognized the potential of the informal communication system in the rural community and "leaked" the news into the system.

Informal communication to the community is another good avenue for attracting visitors to the church. A contagious congregation has celebrative worship services and relevant sermons. When the people of a congregation start speaking positively about their pastor, their church, and their worship, many people become interested and are attracted to the church. This is especially effective if it is natural, spontaneous, and informal. The rural setting is ideal for this strategy of church growth.

The communication network of the rural church can also provide several challenges. How can a rural church reestablish strong small groups? The problem isn't the groups—it's that the communication network has shifted from weekly gatherings to the telephone lines. If small groups have died out as communication forums, perhaps a new purpose for them could be as Bible studies or Christian mission groups that are specifically task-oriented. Men's Bible breakfasts, ladies' prayer circles, and couples' home Bible studies are just a few of the small groups that are thriving in hundreds of rural churches. These churches have redesigned the purpose of the small group.

One of the challenges that faces the rural church with an informal communication system is that the outsiders are not included. Sometimes this can be the pastor. A new pastor at a rural church shook his head in frustration because he was the last to discover that one of the members of the youth group had been gored by a bull. When that pastor begins to hear the news sooner, he will know that he is becoming an insider. As a rural church grows in size, and especially as outsiders are added to the membership, formal communication must become part of the ministry so that all people are informed.

The high velocity of communication around the rural community is a real asset to a growing church. But when things turn sour, it becomes a liability. When the church is stagnant or declining or when there is a negative tone about an important issue, the communication system quickly becomes a deterrent to the church's growth in the community. A congregation, like an individual, can quickly get a bad reputation in the community. To avoid this, church leaders should help the people of the congregation see that their role in communication is important. Every family has its problems, including the family of God. Before anyone hangs the family's dirty laundry out for all to see, it is important to carefully consider the consequences toward Christ and His Church.

4. *Strong loyalty to the home church.* Since the rural church often consists of strong family units who have lived in the area for generations, there exists a strong loyalty to the church. Strong loyalty to a church leads to a healthy pride. It is a good place to begin building a positive image for people who "love their Lord and love their church." People have a strong sense that it is "our church." This is in contrast to congregations in highly mobile areas where it is not uncommon to hear a person talk about their fellow members as "them" instead of "we."

A healthy sense of ownership by church members is important for a church to grow. As people feel ownership in the church, they are more apt to invest their time and talents, their efforts, and their energy.

After a study conducted by the maintenance committee, Jack reported, "We feel that our church must be repainted. It's beginning to look bad. We need to buy the paint, and we need to set a date when we will do it."

The members responded with their yes vote. More significantly, they responded with their money and their energy. When the day to paint came, a large group of the people showed up to help.

Loyalty to the rural church can also provide for some interesting views toward membership. Pastor Johnson, the new pastor at Farrel Church, discovered this when he started visiting all his members. At the Horton home, he found that one son lived 125 miles away and the other lived over 1,000 miles from Farrel. Both had been gone for over three years, so the pastor felt they should be finding church homes where they were. He wrote them, kindly suggesting that they should transfer their membership to churches near their homes. To his amazement, not only did they refuse, but their parents were angered by his attempt to "kick the boys out of the church!"

The strong loyalty factor affected the family's view of membership. Church membership was defined not in the biblical sense of being a part of the Body of Christ but in a formal connection. "The boys would never want to transfer out," their mother explained. "This is their church." She even expressed the hope that the boys might come home someday and take over the family farm.

The healthy and growing church must be sensitive and loving as it makes an attempt to help people see the biblical nature of the church. To provide meaning to membership, many congregations develop a philosophy of ministry. This is a written statement that describes the purpose of the church and what it means to be a member of the church. This document is shared with all prospective members. Before they join, new members are familiar with the membership expectations. Unfortunately, for long-term members who have already established a mind-set of membership loyalty, there is little that can be done directly. Indirectly, the best strategy is to conduct a Bible study on the nature of the church.

The rural church, with its extended family units and loyalty to membership, faces another challenge: dropping someone from the rolls. In all honesty—to God and to one another—every church must do this at one time or another. Amputation is always painful. Yet it is sometimes necessary for a healthy body of Christ. In the rural church it poses some special problems.

Since the rural community represents a population that is less mobile, long-term relationships are common. This makes it more difficult for the members of the congregation to deal with the inactive member. "I've known Vernon for years. He's my neighbor. We've helped each other when things got tough. Back when our barn burned, Vernon helped rebuild it. He wouldn't take any money, either." This assessment of Vernon is that he is a nice person and a longtime friend. But Vernon is also a lapsed Christian. He has been visited by members of the church, and the pastor has talked to him several times, but he does not respond. Christian love includes honesty and discipline, but this can be especially difficult for members of an extended family. It's hard to terminate the membership of your cousin.

There is danger when church membership becomes defined in such a way that it makes no demands, holds no commitment, and therefore, carries no integrity. This is a form of cheap grace that could rightly be called cheap worship or cheap membership. Growing churches are usually churches whose membership integrity is healthy.

There are two sides to God's message—the law with its power to condemn us, and the gospel with its forgiveness. Without one or the other, the whole teaching of God is incomplete. This is what members need to understand about their commitment to Christ and His Church. Once understood, loving but firm ministry to the inactive member is an important fact of life—even if it's your cousin. That's real love.

A tool that many churches use to help establish an integrity of membership for new members is an application for church membership. In many ways the application for church membership will reflect the philosophy of ministry. But it will be more specific about membership expectations. Without being legalistic, the application for church membership simply relates what the congregation has determined are the characteristics of a member of that church.

There is another challenge related to strong home church

loyalty: over a lifetime it may produce a myopic worldview. Some members feel that everyone in the community must know where the church is located, the times of services, the programs that are offered, and "all about the new pastor." Consequently, low priority is given to a suggestion to put up a new sign out front. People wonder why the money should be spent to put a directional sign on the corner. Signs around the church are considered unnecessary, or, worse yet, never considered at all. "Can't they ask if they don't know where the bathroom is?" This is the attitude of one who is on the inside looking out. People who, from one generation to another, are brought to the church by their parents don't know what it's like to be a visitor.

A further aspect of this myopia is the impression that "everyone in this area already belongs to a church." There is hardly a community around any church in the world where that statement would be true. Even it if were true today, it probably wouldn't be true a month from now. Yet many people believe this.

There are a number of ways to look at the church with a broader vision. One way is to gather information from new members soon after they join, asking them what it was like to be a visitor and letting them help the members of the church see the need to be visitor sensitive. Another way is to canvass the community with a simple religious survey about involvement in church. Another way is to encourage church leaders to visit other churches occasionally. This allows them to be a visitor. It also gives them a view of how another church is either sensitive to or oblivious to visitors. It will help them see that the Church is found in many locations. Their worldview is stretched in a healthy way by seeing that the home church to which they are loyal is only one part of the magnificent kingdom of God.

5. *The agricultural calendar is important.* "The church year begins with the start of Advent," explained the new pastor at St. James Church. He was trying to teach the children in his instruction class the importance of the church year. He had only been at the rural church for about a month, and he was appalled at how little the people knew about the church year. Meanwhile, the

people of the church were trying desperately to educate the pastor about the agricultural year.

The leaders of the rural church must be sensitive to this agricultural calendar, which dictates life in the rural community. Most of the programming must revolve around it. In the nonrural community, spring and fall are great times for programs. For the rural church, other times may be better—depending on the nature of the crops, livestock, and gardens in the area.

When crops take precedence, it's usually not a matter of loyalty conflict between the church and mammon. To ask the farmer to attend a church meeting when his crops need harvesting is like asking the preacher to go fishing on Sunday morning. Asking the farmer to attend a committee meeting when the crops need planting is like asking the preacher to attend the same meeting when there is an emergency call to visit a person at the hospital. There is an important difference between a life-style priority and a temporary priority.

The delinquent member of the church has a life-style priority. Everything else is more important than the church. But the farmer's dilemma is seasonal. It is an occasional disruption that requires a temporary change of priorities. Admittedly, it can become a habit. The farmer, like any self-employed businessman, can always find work to do—and use that as an excuse. But the issue here is the occasional need that is beyond his control. Programming in the rural church must be sensitive to the agricultural schedule. Sometimes that is very hard to predict—to the day. Consequently, the rural church calendar should remain flexible during those general times of year when agricultural demands might dictate a change.

Most denominational programming and resources are not geared to the agricultural calendar. The rural church can profit from these materials by adapting them to the rural scene.

The giving of a rural congregation cannot be monitored accurately from Sunday to Sunday as in nonrural churches. In the latter, the first of the year through Easter is a good time financially for the church. In many rural communities (in the Northern Hemisphere) much of the rural money goes toward seed and fertilizer during this time. The whole picture of finances is complicated by the fact that many farmers store their grain for a better market price. For those with livestock, the buying and selling of cattle is often based on the market. Thus rural church income may jump up and down from week to week. This may make it difficult to plan, but for rural people that is a way of life. For the rural church it is a fact of life.

Another important aspect of rural life is the weather. In general, rural churches have good attendance on days when the weather is poor because the people can't get into the fields. During planting and harvesting seasons, the rural church must be sensitive to the weather conditions. One church put it in the bulletin like this: "The Session will meet Wednesday evening, unless it's dry between now and then. In that case the fields can be worked and there will be no Session. Instead, it will meet the first weekday afterward on which it rains."

The time of day is related to the agricultural calendar. In a church consisting of businessmen, men's Bible breakfasts are very popular. In a community of dairy farmers, such a breakfast would have to be held very early or very late. A noon luncheon is probably the best strategy. Likewise, evening meetings may have to start late and end early in the rural community. One church decided that the best time for a meeting was after church on Sunday. Once each month, church was followed by a carry-in dinner and a meeting. Each community will be different, but in every case the agricultural calendar will be an important aspect of rural programming.

6. *Independent nature of the rural individual.* Life in the agricultural community has created rugged individualism in the rural resident. The demands of the work have spawned an independent spirit. Farming is frequently considered the most hazardous occupation. This is due in part to the use of heavy machinery. Another factor is that agricultural people often work alone. Even though the rural family is often a good example of teamwork, many of the members are working at chores by themselves. Independence is a way of life.

"Phyllis, I heard you haven't been feeling well," the pastor casually mentioned.

"Yes, Pastor, I had surgery last week. I was in the hospital in town for four days."

"You were?" the pastor exclaimed in astonishment.

Phyllis, sensing the pastor's discomfort, shared an honest explanation that he would probably never understand: "I just didn't want to bother anybody." Phyllis was following the pattern she had learned well all those years on the farm—she didn't want to bother anybody.

This characteristic of the rural person has significant implications for the rural church. It is a great tribute to thousands of rural churches that have experienced all kinds of hardships and yet survive. What's more, they do it on their own. The independent spirit of the rural church provides it with great stamina. Some rural churches have undergone splits or losses of members but still survive. They held on for years when other churches would have died.

But this independent spirit carries with it some significant challenges. It is hard to build community with a group of independent individuals. It can be difficult to cultivate a cooperative spirit. Sometimes, independent individuals are elected to boards and committees but find it hard to sit through a meeting in which everyone is supposed to discuss the issues and then decide by majority vote.

On the farm—especially the smaller farm—the rural person makes all his own decisions. He doesn't have to ask anyone. There are no meetings. There is no vote. Group process is nonexistent. On larger farms that style has to change. The same is true for the growing church that wants to be effective.

Just three years ago Jim's church averaged 35 people in worship on Sunday morning. Now 125 people worship on the average Sunday. What Jim doesn't realize is that the church has changed. It is not just a larger church. It is a different church. The spirit of independence that was an asset in the days when 35 people came to a comfortable, sleepy church is now a liability in a vibrant, cooperative ministry. That will require a change in Jim's Christian life-style. It will make him feel uncomfortable for a long time.

The cooperative nature of a growing church is also reflected in the need for long-range planning. In the "old days," the board on which Jim sits met whenever they felt *they* had to meet. Now, the governing board of the church wants them to meet every month and be ready to give a report as well. This goes against Jim's independent spirit.

This independence may affect the attitude the church will have toward the denomination. One church that was having problems with the pastor was visited by a regional executive from the denomination. Instead of finding a grateful congregation, the executive was greeted with strong feelings of interference.

Rural individualism can also severely limit possibilities for interchurch cooperation. Many rural churches exist side by side for decades and are never involved in joint projects. To expect an ecumenical spirit among most rural churches is as absurd as suggesting an agricultural labor union—for most of the same reasons.

Some rural pastors make the mistake of believing they have a yoked parish or a dual parish. What they really have is a yoked or dual ministry to two parishes—at least from the standpoint of the people.

If a rural church is going to grow, the positive aspects of the independent spirit must be maximized. Perhaps the best antidote to the challenges faced in this area is the biblical study of spiritual gifts. As a congregation begins to understand and exercise spiritual gifts, a new *interdependent* spirit emerges. On the one hand, the people begin to recognize that each one has been given at least one gift and that every Christian is special and unique in the sight of God. That is the *independent* aspect of gifts. On the other hand, a proper understanding of gifts recognizes that the Body of Christ is a teamwork structure. Each part works in harmony with every other part. The body is only a body as all the gifts function together underneath Christ, who is the Head. This is the *interdependent* aspect of gifts.

Once the independent strengths of rural Christians are harnessed in an interdependent ministry, the church becomes a powerful force for Christ in the community. The church will also become a contagious community, with each person working in harmony with others. This will attract others who see God at work among His people. The end result is that the church will grow.

7. *Rural financial world.* A nonrural person might visualize rural finances as a large wad of dollar bills stuffed in a cookie jar or under the mattress. What a misconception that is. Agricultural economics is a complicated, sophisticated business. The financial world of the rural person is complex. The finances of the farmer may include borrowing, lending, a disbursement of funds to family shareholders in the farm corporation, tax advantages, and depreciation schedules that would boggle the average nonrural householder's mind. It is common to see computers as much a part of the professional farm operation as a tractor or a plow. This is especially true where the trend is toward larger farms with more acres, more cattle, more hired help, bigger machinery, more storage, and more bills to pay. Even the small farmer has complicated financial decisions to make several times each year.

Since the farm is a business with several activities going on at the same time, the self-employed farmer will probably have a good idea of financial management. He understands cash flow during certain periods of time. He also can see the need for expansion and improvement. What a blessing it is that the Lord used agricultural language like the sower and the harvest and the production of fruit. These aspects of biblical teaching can be related to the work of the church in terms to which people in the agricultural community can relate. They also know the cost of bringing in the harvest. This can be beneficial for the growing rural church.

Helping the rural person develop a financial giving pattern that is according to God's will is much more challenging.

"How did you like the pastor's stewardship meetings?" Frank asked Joe.

"Well, I'll tell you, Frank. I'm not arguing against that 10 percent giving idea. After all, it's in the Bible. But as a farmer, how do you decide that? Ten percent of what? I lost money the last five years."

Joe is only telling half the story. Frank knows it, because he's a farmer too. God knows it also! Joe and Frank, like others who are self-employed, can put massive amounts of money back into the business to improve and expand. The result is that they show a loss and don't pay taxes. The government provides for such a system because it generates a healthy economy. Meanwhile, Frank and Joe become wealthier and wealthier. Their assets are not liquid, but they are there, and they usually grow each year.

The rural church that wants to grow must help self-employed farmers see that whatever percentage of income they choose to give to the Lord, it should be from the firstfruits—off the top. This is the Lord's system, and He blesses it. It also unleashes enormous financial power for the rural church.

In some rural areas, the church invites the people to plant the "Lord's acre." A certain number of acres (or a certain number of cattle) are designated, and at market time that portion goes to the Lord.

Some rural congregations have a church farm. This is usually a parcel of land that was given to the church in a will. It is rented out, or it can be farmed by the members. In either case, the income can be used to help supplement the mission of the church. It is a plan that runs the risk of discouraging the regular offerings of the people. Therefore, it is best to designate this income for a special outreach project.

Rural people are generous by nature. They can and will be generous to the Lord and His work, but they must be trained in good principles of biblical stewardship. Denominational stewardship material geared to the rural scene should be available to the rural church, but more is needed than stewardship education.

Any church that is highly involved in outreach, mission, and church growth will have a better sense of financial giving. As a church responds to the Great Commission, the people seem to come alive with a "growth consciousness." This attitude stimulates more sacrificial giving. This is true in all churches, and the rural church is no exception.

As farmers accumulate more land, their estate grows larger. The rural church should consider developing a foundation to which farmers could leave a portion of their estate. By remembering the church in their will, the family is making a provision for returning to the Lord a portion of the blessings He has given to them.

One caution is in order. Many churches build an endowment fund that serves as a false life-support system. This is dangerous, and it becomes a crutch for the church. It also undermines the faith adventure aspect of giving. This can be avoided by developing a foundation that has certain mission goals. For example, a large percentage of all gifts would be given to a mission outreach project designated by the congregation. The balance must be used by the congregation for outreach locally. It is also important to put a time limit by which the money must be spent.

Another financial fact in the rural church is that many people have wealth that isn't liquid. Many have a lot of their cash already tied up in some way. Therefore, the rural church should also stress the stewardship of time and talents. Agricultural people work hard. During certain times of the year, their work cannot be interrupted. But during the "slow" times, the farmer has more discretionary time than the nonrural person who punches a time clock. During the right times, the rural church has a tremendous potential for available workers. The church that wants to be effective and grow will use these God-given blessings.

8. *Sometimes the rural rate of change is slower.* Change is neither good nor bad. It carries no value in and of itself. In the rural community change is often slower. Some people boast that they live in the same town in which they were born. In the rural community many people are like Ralph who says, "I sleep in the same room in which I was born." And Ralph is 63 years old.

Yet the rate of change itself is changing. Mobility and media exposure are bringing change more rapidly to the rural community. Some people remember when Grandma Schmidt first got a set of plastic dishes. It was three years after they were first introduced through the mail-order catalog. Last week her son installed a dish antenna that linked the television in the farmhouse to a satellite.

Change is hard for all people. We are creatures of habit, and anything that changes a habit makes us uncomfortable. In the rural church, change may be more difficult for the old-timers of the community. They may be more conservative in their attitude toward change. If the younger people want change, it is important to be sensitive to the older members for whom the experience may be difficult.

One of the best ways to help people accept change is to bring them on board early in the process. The church that successfully handles change is the church that helps people develop ownership. Getting everyone involved is the key. This can be accomplished by providing an open atmosphere in which anyone can feel free to disagree. People should understand that they can disagree without being disagreeable.

Information is important. People need to be informed about what's happening. In a growing church, the subtle challenge is to continually discover, "Who are we?" When the rural church grows, it often grows with the addition of nonrural people. This causes what is commonly called the "pioneer-homesteader conflict." Those in control are feeling invaded by people who are new and different. The uncomfortable feelings of change may be especially acute for the rural person who has lived a life of little change.

Reality orientation is the technique whereby the leaders of the church help the people see who they are. Some people might think, Oh, we are just a small church. In reality, the church may be larger than 60 percent of the churches in the denomination. One of the key methods of reality orientation is to show graphs of where the church is going and where it stands in various categories. These can be compared with graphs of the previous years.

9. *The reality of risk.* The rural person knows about risk. Agriculture is a business of risk. One depends on two of the most volatile and unreliable aspects of life: the weather and the market.

Risk is a way of life in the rural community. The people live with it every year. Should I plant early or a little later? Should I sell these sheep this week or wait? Is this combine really going to make enough of a difference to pay for itself over the years?

Should I use this herbicide or that one? How should it be applied? Each year brings thousands of difficult questions. Many of them have unpredictable answers.

This characteristic of the rural community can be an asset to the church. Growing, effective churches are not just churches with gimmicks. They are primarily churches on a faith adventure. They are churches made up of people who trust God for His promises. It isn't "church as usual" as a group of people go through the motions. God is alive in a growing church. The people are alive in Christ.

Christ calls people to walk by faith, not by sight. The Holy Spirit, by His nature, calls people to take a leap of faith. It can be an uncomfortable life-style of insecurity. Yet, for rural people, insecurity is a way of life.

The rural church can tap that willingness to risk and that boldness of faith and use it not only to help people plant cotton or harvest apples or raise cattle but also to plant churches, harvest Christians, and raise disciples. It takes faith in God and, in the proper sense, in oneself. If that willingness to step out in faith can be harnessed in the rural church, a tremendous force for the growth of the Kingdom can be unleashed.

The people at a church in Farmington had been faced with the need to build for six months when they called all their people together for a business meeting. "We need to build," said Tim. "We know that. But we also know it will cost $100,000. It's been a hard year for farmers the last two years. Two years ago we had terrible weather, and last year we had great weather, but the prices were so low it didn't pay to plant. But we need to make a decision now. What do you think?"

"I think we should go for it," said Phil. "After all, next year is bound to be better."

It's that kind of faith in God, hope for the future, and willingness to risk that will pull the farmer to the fields like a magnet. It's that kind of faith that gives rural people a willingness to move forward with boldness in mission and ministry. Properly directed, it is the risk-taking spiritual adventure that allows the Lord of the harvest to send laborers into His harvest.

10. *Pragmatism.* Rural people are not high on theory. They do not spend much time in speculation. They are practical people who live off the land. Those who do it well do not spend a lot of time dreaming philosophy. They see the job. They calculate the best way to accomplish it. They do it the cheapest way with the least amount of effort.

When it comes to the rural church, the people are very pragmatic in their approach. They won't tolerate a minister who is purely academic. They do not accept denominational programs that are impractical.

Because of this, rural people are good stewards of the limited resources God has given them. What they accomplish with the limited resources of money and people is usually more efficient than churches among other types of people. The rural church is not wasteful with its resources. Buildings are functional. Programs are useful. Expenditures are realistic.

Church growth is really a matter of good stewardship. How can the church use its limited resources most effectively in meeting the challenge to make disciples? As the pragmatic rural church develops strategies along these lines, its very tone of practicality will develop receptivity among those in the community who are unchurched.

Rural people help churches become and remain effective in the task God has given all His people: to go into the harvest in order to make disciples of all peoples.

3

The Rural Rainbow

With thunder still booming in the distance, I looked out over the expanse of dark green cornfield. Beyond the beauty of the rural earth, I saw another beauty—the rainbow. The colors of the rainbow brought to mind the variety of God's creation. As my eyes searched the rural landscape, I was reminded that here, too, is great diversity. A beautiful variety exists among churches that are distinctly rural.

Not every rural church is out in the open—away from a town. Some are near big cities. Some are being invaded. They are changing. But all of them are churches where a significant number of the members are people of the land.

Not every church in every situation can grow in numbers of people, but many can. Many can grow at a faster rate than they are now growing. They can be more effective in helping people grow up and mature in faith. They can be more efficient in their ministry of outreach. Knowing the types of rural churches is important. There is great variety in God's rainbow of rural churches. Each is unique in some way—even though they share a rural mind-set.

No church can be categorized 100 percent. Types will overlap, but generally speaking, there are 10 categories of churches on the rural landscape. These churches are each unique by their definitions. Each has its own possibilities for ministry. These 10 types of rural churches are given to reveal the variety in God's creation, to thrust laborers into the harvest that surrounds them, and to emphasize the privilege of sharing in the harvest.

1. *The cornfield church.* This is the classic stereotype of the rural church. It may be a white frame building or brick, but it is

located in a landscape of great expanses of land. The fields may be corn or cotton fields, vineyards or rangeland. This is the open, country church. By its definition, this church is surrounded by land that is sparsely populated.

Even in the cornfield church not all the people are strictly rural in the sense that they are in agribusiness. Yet the majority are farmers, ranchers, or involved in some other form of agribusiness. They set the tone and life-style for the rural church.

The cemetery is usually located nearby—either beside the church or behind it. The parsonage is next door. Often there is a fellowship hall in the basement of the church or next door. There may be a one-room school building that serves as a symbol of days gone by when children walked several miles to school. It is a church with a strong self-image as a country church.

Often the cornfield church is part of a dual ministry, with the pastor serving another church, perhaps several others. The church may have declined in attendance because the area population has dwindled. Sometimes the church is subsidized by the denomination.

The church serves as the community focal point for many of the folks in the area. There is a long history. Members have many relatives buried in the cemetery. The church is part of their lives. This is their church, and they are proud of it.

As farmers expand their acreage, they purchase one farm after another. They generally sell off the farmhouse with a few acres. The people who buy these houses are usually people who have moved from towns or cities in order to live in the country. They are becoming country people, but they will never be rural people.

When people move to a new house, they are more receptive to a new church than at other times in their lives. They are starting a new adventure in the country. They are ready to meet friends, try new things, and if invited, perhaps visit a new church. If they find a welcome and friendly people, they will probably be very responsive.

There are other people in the rural area who have not been reached. They may not be as receptive as the newcomers. Yet, with changes in their lives, their receptivity will increase. There may be a death in the family, an illness, or problems. If the church is sensitive, loving, and helpful, the deeds done in genuine love may serve as bridges over which the good news of Jesus Christ can reach them.

Though the growth of the cornfield church is limited, most churches of this type can grow. There are few places where almost all the local people go to church.

The cornfield church has another opportunity for growth. There are communities that do not have a church. Could the cornfield church plant a church in one of these places? Often there are kinship ties in other small towns in the area. Relatives of members could be the nucleus of a new church in their own community. The place to begin is stretching the vision of the membership to see the opportunities that exist.

2. *The county seat church.* This church is located in the county seat or is situated in a small but central industrial or service area of the general region. Often it is located not too far from a town square. It is highly visible, and its location is well-known by people from the area because they have been to the town for business at one time or another.

The county seat church often has a large structure and a long tradition. The worship life may be more formal than the cornfield church. The form of government may be more structured.

Most of the people who belong to the church are farmers. Though many of the members and the townspeople don't see the church as rural, it reflects the rural mind-set of the majority of its members. Those members not of a rural orientation have been drawn to the church because they have located in the area for vocational reasons. This includes the sheriff's deputy and his family, the family that runs the market, and the county commissioner.

The county seat church has great opportunities for growth. It is a church that could use direct mail. It is a church that can get involved in county events. It can be highly visible in the regional newspaper.

3. *The small town church.* This rural church is different from the previous type of church in that it does not share the regional flavor and the countywide visibility that is part of most county

seat churches. The small town church is located in or near a town with a fairly stable population of 350 to 2,500. The building may be more modern in architecture than the cornfield church. Its design and some of the programming have been affected by a town mentality, but only to a degree. In the rural small town church, the majority of people are agricultural. Some of the farmers have retired and moved to smaller homes in town, but their rural orientation is still with them—much stronger than the garden in the backyard would indicate.

One of the unique aspects of this type of church is its flexible tradition. Since the church has some townspeople, is faced with challenges in the town setting, and usually has a more modern setting, there tends to be more flexibility than in the cornfield church and the county seat church. This helps the church meet some of the specific challenges and opportunities for growth that it faces.

The small town church, like the county seat church, usually has a larger potential harvest than the cornfield church. Probably there is at least one other church in its area. This makes the philosophy of ministry an especially important aspect of the small town church. What is it that makes this church unique? What are its priorities?

The small town church that wants to grow will carefully discover the felt needs of the people around them. Are there needs for family counseling? Is there a desire for youth work? Does the town need a church with a strong program of Christian education? Are there people with physical needs that the church could meet? Once the church discovers the needs, then it must choose which ones it can meet and develop a ministry to meet those needs. This philosophy of ministry could be a document articulating the priorities for ministry. It can be used to inform the community of what makes this church unique.

Large cities and suburbs of major metropolitan areas often use welcoming groups and visit each new family. This is often lacking in a small town. This may be a ministry in which the small town church can get involved. It is an excellent source for future outreach.

The small town church should not limit its outreach to the people of the town. It is possible that there are country rural people who couldn't fit in the cornfield church—or who weren't accepted. What about the person who is divorced or one who has been in trouble with the law? His fellow church members and family members at the cornfield church may forgive him, but he may still feel uncomfortable with them. There is also the person who never felt comfortable with the philosophy of ministry of the cornfield church. These people are all prospects for the small town church serious about the Great Commission.

What about people in other small towns? Rural people in most areas are accustomed to traveling. These people may think nothing of traveling to a neighboring town to go to church. Even if their own town has a church of their denomination, they may prefer to worship in another town because of the philosophy of ministry of the church there. If there are people who care enough about a rural church to commute to another town, they could form a nucleus for a rural small town church to be planted in their town. It is not uncommon to find the small town church thinking far too small when it comes to outreach possibilities.

4. *The solo church.* Sometimes a church is the only church in or near a small town or in a general region. When the majority of the members are agriculturally oriented and set the tone for the church, it is a rural solo church.

A church may be a solo church through a variety of circumstances. A church can become a solo church because other churches in the area have closed. This is one of the most challenging situations for a solo church. The church must recognize first of all that it has *become* a solo church. For those churches who have always been a solo church, the mentality of being the only church in the area is part of the tradition. But as a new role for a rural church, it requires rethinking the philosophy of ministry. Through the closure of other congregations, the church now stands alone. No one in the congregation decided to change the nature of the church in its relationship to the community, but it happened. How will the church serve the community now that it is God's *only* representative Christian family present? What about those people who belonged to the other churches? The new solo church has a great opportunity and a Christian responsibility to reach these folks and integrate them into their Christian community.

The members of the congregation that suddenly become a solo church need help to change their local worldview. The change will affect programming, evangelistic outreach, publicity, and ministry to those in physical need. For a church traditionally alone in an area, these aspects of Christian worldview and congregational life-style are inherited. For the new solo church, they represent significant changes. That is one of the greatest challenges before the congregation that suddenly finds itself in the solo church position.

Another challenge is the important question, "Why did the other congregations die?" The related question is, "What can we learn about the health, vitality, and longevity of our own church?"

What are the facts? For the new solo church, it is essential that they gather as much correct information as possible. Proper diagnosis is necessary. One of the best methods is by interviewing the people from these other churches. The solo church will gather the facts and apply that knowledge to its own ministry.

A church may be a solo church because the people of the area have been unreceptive to the gospel. This has great significance for the church that is God's only outpost. This field one day will turn receptive—ripe for the harvest.

The church should follow the strategy my wife uses with her strawberry patch. Strawberries aren't good before they ripen, but once they do become ripe, they can spoil and become full of bugs very rapidly. So she monitors her strawberries, checking them each day. I don't bother to check them because I know I'll be recruited when the time is right. Likewise, the solo church in an unreceptive area should watch for those signs of a ripening harvest. Not everyone must be involved in monitoring—others can be recruited when the time is right.

How do you check receptivity? An occasional religious survey is one way. Another way is to monitor the number of visitors to the church. If there is a growing number of visitors, ask, "Who are these people? Are they from a particular area? Are they a certain kind of people in our ministry area? Do they represent a growing receptivity to the gospel?"

One church monitored receptivity by sending a direct mail appeal to all the residents of the area. Twice a year, at Easter and Christmas, they sent out an invitation to their worship services. They included a reply card that gave the people opportunity to indicate that they wanted the church to pray for them. The number of visitors and the number of prayer requests that are received each year are an indication of the receptivity of people in the area who will respond to that method of outreach.

A third reason for a solo church is that the population is perceived as being too small to support a second church. While this may be true of certain areas, it is not the situation in most places. Most church growth experts agree the world needs many more churches. Often they will be new, small churches without elaborate buildings or full-time ordained ministers. But they are needed.

It is important for the solo church to be aware of population trends. Local government offices in the majority of regions have census information. The church should track the population of its ministry area every year—and monitor the changes. Usually school boards, bankers, and real estate agents have good information about the movement of people. If the population is compared to the membership figures of the solo church, it is easy to predict the number of unchurched people in the area. If that number grows larger, the solo church can start new churches or invite a denomination or mission agency to do so.

Another factor contributing to the solo church phenomenon is that an area may be populated by ethnic groups who create cultural barriers other denominations are unable or unwilling to cross. The solo church will not be attractive to all types and groups of people. Still these people are the evangelistic responsibility of the solo church.

The solo church in a multiethnic area should open its doors wide to all the people. It should be known as a friendly church.

There will be those who, because of ethnic distance, find it too uncomfortable to join the solo church. In this case, a strategy should be developed to start fellowship Bible studies among the ethnic group. These fellowships could provide a bridge to membership in the solo church, or they may become the seeds of a new church in that ethnic group. In either case, it is the people themselves who will determine which way the fellowship will go.

A Christian community might be a solo church because it is the first church in a frontier area. In certain parts of the world, the population is very minimal. When land is cleared for agricultural use or previously restricted land is opened by the government, rural people begin populating the area. The first church is a solo church. One of the characteristics of such a setting is that the congregation is a solo church only temporarily.

If the vision for other churches is strong, and churches are likely to develop rather quickly, then the solo church needs to look beyond its unique, temporary characteristic. Long-range planning should be made with the view that soon there will be other churches in the area.

The solo church has an image that represents the visible presence of God to the entire community. Consequently, it will minister to many people beyond its membership—at least on an occasional basis. People will come to the solo church for physical help because it's the only church around. Counseling will include many who are not members. Anyone in the area who is seeking a church wedding or funeral will come to the solo church. The minister of the solo church may represent all Christians of the area at many of the regional functions. There are many great opportunities for the solo church to present the gospel to the people in the area.

The solo church may be more cosmopolitan in its style of worship, programs, and doctrinal priorities. Since it is the only church in a large area, it will be composed of people from more than one tradition. It will reflect a certain rural mind-set, but within that framework a diversity of life-styles and worldviews may be found.

For the solo church faced with long distances between

towns in the area, the planting of satellite churches may provide a good strategy for making disciples. A satellite church can be described as an extension or branch of the main church. The minister of the solo church also pastors the satellite churches. A lay assistant or assistant minister may take over the satellite church when it is big enough. Another approach would be to plant independent churches throughout the region. These churches are started by the solo church, but the apron strings are cut as soon as the new churches can stand on their own.

5. *The playground church.* The rural church found in a resort area is a playground church. This church can be surrounded by lakes with cottages, mountains for skiing, or just beautiful scenery for sight-seeing. There is a fluctuation in population during different times of the year. Sometimes this fluctuation is only short-term. Perhaps people are in the area for the weekend or for a week or two. Sometimes the church is surrounded by people who are long-term but not permanent residents. These are people who are in the area for an entire season. There is a third type of population that is short-term and long-term. These are the folks that inhabit the area around the playground church every weekend for a season. They are often people who live in large cities or suburban areas not too far away. They migrate every weekend from their home environment to a cottage they either own or rent.

The rural playground church has a real challenge. People escaping for rest and relaxation, fun and games, often are escaping from all their routines—including church. The church that reaches out and invites these people will have many visitors, especially during the peak play season.

Most of the visitors who come to the rural playground church will not be people with a rural mentality. However, they will not be threatening to the local church members because they are temporary attenders.

This church is often characterized by a casual dress code. Less-structured worship forms may be used. Some are drive-in churches where visitors can stay in their cars. The playground church conducts worship services in campgrounds, on beaches, around campfires, and in parks. This is an important ministry, and it is an essential part of the Great Commission *if* the goal is discipleship.

Discipleship means working with people so that God can move them to responsible membership in the Body of Christ. This is a challenge among people who are only temporarily on the scene. If these people are going to be reached for discipleship, a follow-up ministry is important. Follow-through is always essential if disciples are to be made, but the task is more difficult if they are visitors to the playground, and will require contacts with a church in their home area. As long as they are permanent residents elsewhere, this follow-up strategy will be necessary. ·

With this type of evangelism the playground church may not be showing significant growth itself but may indeed be a vital ministry for the growth of the Kingdom.

Another outreach ministry of the rural playground church is the "second home church" development. This is a strategy to start a seasonal church among people who are long-term, non-permanent residents. These are usually not rural people, and they may form a people group of their own who share a common life-style. They may be skiers or hunters or fishermen. They may be identified by the local people as "boaters" or "lake people." Some good human resources for second home church development include seminary students, retired ministers, or Christian laypeople from that group.

6. *The shrinking church.* The rural church classified as a shrinking church is by definition located in a community or area that is running out of people. It is actually a shrinking community. This happens in some rural areas because farms are larger and farmers are fewer. If the area does not have a diversified economy based on diversified resources, the people begin to look for employment elsewhere.

Theoretically, a church can grow, even if the population is declining. However, that is an exceptional situation and only temporary—especially if the population trend continues away from the area. The shrinking church and the community often go through the stages of death. People can be angry. They may deny the reality of death. The congregation begins to feel over-churched in buildings and underchurched in ministry. The maintenance of the church plant may become a burden in the face of a dwindling support base. It may become increasingly difficult to keep a pastor. Churches may be yoked together into a dual parish where the pastor serves two congregations.

The rural congregation of a shrinking church has an important ministry—a ministry of hope that goes beyond depression, love that surpasses despair, and life that transcends death itself. Ministry in a shrinking community is an opportunity to share the Good News with people who are surrounded with bad news. The worship service in the church should be a celebration of joy and peace that goes beyond human understanding.

For the rural church in a shrinking community, weekly worship can become a weekly love song. The dwindling members can come together and share strength, fellowship, and common concerns. The church that believes the promise of the Great Commission recognizes that the Lord is with His people always . . . in all their days.

It will also be a church that faces difficult situations with possibility thinking. A realistic and positive Christian attitude is one that attracts people—especially those who hurt. The shrinking church may be able to win to Jesus Christ people who have never been receptive before. Adversity often stimulates openness to the gospel. Unchurched members of the community are good prospects for the gospel as it is presented in the context of a genuine ministry to their needs.

The shrinking church may die one day, yet its people need to have a perspective of ministry that is biblical. People are like grass—they come and go. Churches are like seasons, they flourish and sometimes, for reasons beyond their control, they die. The Lord reaches people for eternity through people and churches that come and go. The lasting value of the church is not the earthly membership roll or the stately building but the changing of lives, the making of disciples.

The shrinking church ought to make out a spiritual will. Whatever resources are left can be forwarded to a new mission in a corner of the Kingdom that is growing. Every person needs a rite of passage to understand the big events of life. The comprehension of the death of a church is no different. A rite of passage event is necessary for the people. One church had a big celebration service, thanking God for all the years of ministry in that place. They invited all the people who had previously attended that church. It was a great homecoming. It was their last "hurrah!"

7. *The metro-satellite church.* The rural congregation that is a metro-satellite church is undergoing enormous change. It is located near a large metropolitan area. It is reached by traveling out from the city, through the suburbs, through some expanses of unpopulated land, into the area of a satellite community. In order to survive as a metro-satellite community, there must be good transportation facilities into the metropolitan job market.

The metro-satellite community is experiencing the enormous challenges of rurbia—a rural area invaded by urban refugees. The congregation of a metro-satellite church is facing a great influx of people. If it chooses to remain rural, it will ultimately become an isolated oddity of one kind of people in a mass of other kinds of people. It will stick out like a sore thumb. It may eventually die. If it chooses to change and accept the new population, it will lose its distinction as a rural church. For the church that wants to reach people for Jesus Christ and bring them into the existing fellowship, death as a distinctly rural church is imminent.

The metro-satellite church that reaches out will grow rapidly. Much of it will be transfer growth. It will face the challenge of assimilating these new members. It will also inevitably face the pioneer-homesteader range war. There will be tension between newcomers and old-timers, which will frequently include competition for power. It's only a natural reaction, but it must be managed in a rapidly changing church.

The new members of the metro-satellite church are people who have great expectations for their community and toward their new church. These are people who are on their third hop away from what they perceive to be the bad environment of the city. Some of them have fled the city to the suburbs and then have moved again to the satellite community at great cost of time, energy, and money. The breadwinners will travel long distances to get to work.

This trend to move to the country is different from previous trends to move to the city. People who moved to the city had been attracted to the urban area by the need for work. They went to the cities poor. Those fleeing to the metro-satellite communities are people who have made it. They are usually wealthy people who can afford to live where they wish and commute to work. Tens of thousands of these people are creating rurbia in the metro-satellite communities.

The metro-satellite church is growing so fast that the rural mentality is in a state of shock. The rural mind-set is disoriented by the rapid change. Imagine the trauma for folks like Barb and Bill. For 60 years they watched at dawn for the deer that gracefully moved across the open field on the other side of the road. Within six months a shopping center appeared . . . and there are no more deer. The church to which Bill and Barb belong is a rural-style building that has suddenly been surrounded by a landscape of townhouses, new homes, and shops. This church faces the inevitable departure from the world of the rural church.

While the tremendous change creates problems for the metro-satellite church, it brings with it many opportunities. The people who are moving into the area are receptive to change—including a change in their worship life. They are fresh to the community and the church. They have new ideas and bring new energy. If the metro-satellite church will let them, they will revitalize the church.

These new members will bring preconceived ideas about the nature and purpose of the church. The metro-satellite church must assimilate them in a way that includes a reorientation of the philosophy of ministry and the expectations of membership for their new church. They also should be trained to have a Great Commission mentality so that they are sensitive to opportunities for reaching others with the gospel.

8. *The suburban fringe church.* This church is also a phenomenon of rurbia. This scene differs from the metro-satellite church

primarily by the distance from the metropolitan area to the church. The suburban fringe church is reached by leaving the metro area, traveling through the suburbs and reaching the fringe area without passing through any great expanse of sparsely populated land.

The suburban fringe church is characterized by transition. The world around the church is radically changing as streets are widened, fields give way to concrete, and traffic lights dot the major crossroads. The membership of the church is also changing. As a rural church, it will pass into history.

The range war between the homesteaders and the pioneers is also characteristic of this fading rural church. The transition may take place so rapidly that the pioneers don't even know what has happened. They are uncomfortable, threatened, and excited by all the new members. Ministry in this situation is challenging and very important. The pioneers need love and the challenge to accept change. The homesteaders need to learn to be sensitive to the needs of those who have laid the groundwork of ministry for growth. The pioneers have wisdom, experience, and a history in the congregation. The homesteaders bring enthusiasm, new perspective, and energy. Together they form a team that can be a great blessing to their changing church in a rapidly growing community.

One of the challenges for the suburban fringe church is related to its growth, much of which consists of Christians changing churches. Faith United Church is a good example. The pastor is elated about the growing church. The people are proud of the ministry of outreach but in reality, Faith is experiencing primarily transfer growth. There is nothing wrong with transfer growth. Faith Church should thank God for it, but it could be a temptation for the church to relax its evangelistic outreach. The denominational paper recently featured Faith United as a great church growth congregation. But growth of the Kingdom happens as *new* Christians are brought into the Body of Christ. This conversion growth, as it is called, is the cutting edge of Kingdom growth. The suburban fringe church needs to be challenged to see the Great Commission in proper perspective. While the people of the church can and should thank God for the transfer of new blood, strategies need to be added to reach the unchurched. This is difficult for the suburban fringe church because it is preoccupied with the assimilation of new members through transfer growth.

Growth frequently creates another challenge. The church is running out of room; the parking lot is a massive traffic jam; the halls are crowded; and the seating capacity in the sanctuary is pressed to its limits. Eventually the topic of building larger facilities becomes an important issue. Usually the plan to build runs one or two years late. Change is rapid; church government is often slow. Foresight and preplanning are rare. Nevertheless, when the facilities are crowded, the suburban fringe church should build.

Building carries with it some unique challenges. The enormous amount of time, energy, and money required to build is a drain on the congregation. Often it will take the focus away from outreach and turn it inward. This is a great danger and should be avoided.

Staffing is another problem for the growing, changing suburban fringe church. What many congregations fail to realize is that their most valuable asset is not the land or buildings; it is their staff. The church will need to provide the buildings for growth, but not at the expense of staff growth. Few churches staff for growth. The church grows and the congregation takes slow steps toward adding staff. The church that staffs for growth will *anticipate* growth and plan its staffing accordingly.

9. *The migrant church.* This rural church is unique because it consists of migrant farm workers. Migrant workers are a significant part of the agricultural scenery in many areas. This rural church can take two forms. It can be a temporary church that ministers to each wave of migrant workers as they come into the area. Or it can be mobile and part of the migrant group—traveling when it travels. The second model is more effective because these sojourners can build a sense of community through this mobile church.

The migrant church usually represents a culture other than the dominant culture of the people of the surrounding area. The best strategy for this type of mission is to train one or more of the migrants to be the pastors of the group. This has several advantages. First, the pastors go with the migrants when they go. Second, they are from the migrant group and therefore represent a ministry from the inside. Third, since they are from the inside, they speak the language, live the life-style, share the dreams, and know the hurts better than anyone could from outside the group. Obviously these pastors cannot be seminary-trained people. But with proper lay training, God can bless the ministry in the migrant church.

Evangelistic work among migrants can be very effective. If migrant people are a close-knit group, their loyalties to each other run deep. The migrant community frequently consists of family groups. This can set the stage for a great number of people to gravitate to Christ at the same time, making their responses to the gospel individually, but moving Christward as a group. These conditions make it possible for the rapid growth of a Christian church in this rural setting.

10. *The nonchurch church.* The rural church that is a nonchurch is in every respect a church. The community, however, does not recognize it as a church because it does not have a permanent building. This might also be true of the migrant church. However, migrants often move from camp to camp where permanent buildings are used. When there are no permanent buildings, the migrant church would be primarily identified as migrant and only secondarily called a nonchurch church.

The nonchurch church people often describe themselves as a fellowship. This may be a new church that is located in temporary facilities. Sometimes their type of church is called a chapel or a mission or a preaching station. Perhaps the people have no intention of ever building a permanent building, or maybe they utilize the house-church strategy for Kingdom growth. They, too, would be classified as a nonchurch church.

Many evangelistic strategists have been advocating the nonchurch church style. It saves money because limited resources are not invested in expensive land or buildings. This strategy, although found among rural people (like the Amish), is more prevalent in urban ministry situations.

The electronic church is a form of nonchurch church most common among rural people. This refers to the phenomenon of radio and television preachers who bring religion into the home. For rural people in isolated areas, this may be a reasonable contact with Christianity. It may be a way of finding and reaching receptive people who could respond and eventually be used by God to form a new church in a rural area.

Many denominations are seeking ways to use television as an instructional tool. This is especially true of cable television. At this point in time, most rural people do not have access to cable because of the limitations of distance. However, satellite communication is making television transmission available anywhere in the world. This may soon be a way to reach rural people all over the globe. The nonchurch church could have a great role to play in introducing Jesus Christ to rural people groups.

4

Healing the Church's Wounded Personality

*I*t is common to find a low self-image among people who belong to rural congregations. This is not to say each member has low self-esteem personally. But corporately, as the Body of Christ, the rural church often suffers from a wounded personality.

Depression Factors

The low self-image in rural churches is generated by several factors that are real and felt deeply by rural people. There is no doubt that these factors affect the congregation's growth potential. There are at least five major elements that contribute to this condition.

1. *The denomination.* Most denominational headquarters are located in large metropolitan areas. Consequently, denominational executives live in and around nonrural environments. They attend nonrural churches. As a result, the programs, policies, and the very tone of much that descends from the denominational office is geared toward nonrural people.

What does that say to the rural church? Though not intentional, the message often received is: "You are not important." Consequently, the church that is rural does not respond to denominational programming. This is unfortunate because many rural churches desperately need good programs in education, stewardship, social service, evangelism, church planting, and in congregational health and growth. A critical need in the rural church is programming directed toward dealing with change.

In hundreds of rural areas the out-migration to the cities has continued, but in many areas the trend has reversed. Many people are moving from the cities to rural areas. They are not coming as agricultural people. Many are buying small farms and ranches, but they aren't farming or ranching. They are sometimes called "gentleman farmers" and "hobby ranchers," hiring the work done and enjoying the rural environment. Many of them are attending churches. The mix is difficult, but the opportunities are great.

Every denomination with rural churches should be tuned in to the challenge of providing material to help. In a cooperative spirit, programs can be developed that are sensitive to the rural mind-set and that speak to rural needs. Great Kingdom growth can occur—both in quantity and quality, if denominational people will give guidance. The help will have a positive effect among those who feel like a forgotten group.

2. *Pastors.* Many pastors who serve churches today are people from the rural scene or one generation removed. One would think that would make them excellent rural pastors. It would if they hadn't been sent off to seminary.

While seminary training may have many strong points, one of the greatest liabilities is that it lifts ministerial candidates out of their own culture. Whether that culture is American Indian, Hispanic, Black, or rural, the impact is the same. The deculturalization process has inoculated them from their own culture group. Seminary graduates may look upon the rural scene as foreign territory. It's a nice place to visit, but who would want to live there? Rural congregations get the message no matter how subtle or how unintentional it might be.

There tends to be an attitude among many pastors that moving up the ladder means moving to a big city or suburban church. One pastor left a large city church in order to take on a floundering rural church. Some of his colleagues asked him what he had done wrong to deserve that. This debilitating attitude reaches the rural church and results in a negative self-image.

Many pastors who are called to their first work at a rural church see it merely as a stepping-stone. "Well, I guess everyone has to start somewhere," remarked the young graduate as he looked at his first assignment to a rural church.

The attitude that the rural church is second rate permeates

the pastoral structure and has several side effects. One is that rural churches frequently have to be content with a retiring pastor who wants to slow down and take it easy. So he goes to a rural (usually also small) church. Or some of those pastors who can't make it in other ministries are placed in rural areas. Therefore, many rural churches are saddled with ecclesiastical flunkies. Another side effect is long pastoral vacancies.

Pastoral attitudes toward rural ministry need to be changed. With some of the recent out-migration from cities, the rural areas should be considered great lands of opportunity. The self-worth of the rural church can be improved considerably if seminaries and denominations would begin giving a better image to rural opportunities. Often the rural church is considered conservative (in the bad sense of antiprogressive), backward, and out of touch. This is a naive image of rural people who are very sophisticated and willing to grow—if they are led.

Denominations would do well to send their best people to rural churches with great potential. These ministers could serve as models to others. This would be a great benefit to boost the self-image of the rural church.

3. *The use of yoked ministries.* The rural ministry is often a shared ministry. Pastors serve a dual parish or are circuit riders for several churches. Some are bivocational and work at secular jobs during the week. Rural churches need to recognize that these types of ministries are not poor models. The Lord has blessed these types of arrangements for centuries.

Some rural churches are small and in all probability will stay that way. The population potential isn't there. But in many situations the possibility for numerical growth does exist.

In places where growth is possible, sharing a pastor may be a deterrent to the expansion of the church. Rural people need to be led to think growth. What is needed is a leap of faith to take on a full-time pastor who will lead the congregation to growth. The concern for money is a cynical argument and a tool of the devil. If the church grows, the money will be there to pay for the full-time salary. If the congregation waits until it has the money, then it will not be acting on faith.

Many rural churches are outpriced for full-time pastoral work simply because denominational policies require a fully trained, seminary graduate. This method has no biblical precedent. Someone has said that to require eight years of seminary training as the *only* way to enter the ministry is one of the greatest deterrents to church growth.

4. *Growth stagnation.* Unpainted barns, vacant farmhouses, and shrinking towns are sometimes a part of rural reality. Where these exist, the rural church is declining and depressed.

This is a difficult factor to deal with because it is beyond anybody's control. It is usually temporary. It may take several decades, but one day it will change. This is especially true for those places where urban out-migration is in the future population picture.

Meanwhile, the rural church in a declining population ought to look at world mission. Pastors and denominational leaders can help people focus on the privilege of being world Christians. If they cannot grow where they are, they can support missions in growing areas around the world.

Pastoral care is very important in this situation. There are instances where yoking congregations together or consolidating churches will be necessary, but this should be a last resort. History shows that when two congregations merge, the new church ends up about the size of the larger of the two churches before they merged. In other words, merger often promotes decline.

5. *Big is beautiful.* Smallness does not make a church rural, but many rural churches are small in size. Unfortunately some people believe the rural church must remain small. This is not the case. This is a nongrowth excuse. It is a mentality that enslaves the small rural church in the prison of mediocrity. Many rural churches are small because they are structured *against* growth. They fail to plan and work for growth.

There is a tendency to perpetuate the idea that big is beautiful. This has a negative effect on the small church and promotes the opposite principle: Small must be ugly. This is not true in God's eyes. It's not true according to church growth experts either.

Many people believe church growth means that churches must get bigger and bigger. They understand the superchurch to be the church growth ideal. This is a gross error. Church growth declares that the fastest way God's kingdom grows is by church planting. Church growth people call for planting thousands of new, small churches around the world.

Small is ugly only when it is contrary to the will of God. If a church allows roadblocks to hinder receptive people from joining the church, then it is an ugly situation. If a church is seeking God's will but can't grow numerically because people are simply not there, then small is what is expected. Small can be beautiful!

Building a Positive Image

What can be done to build a sense of corporate self-worth in the rural church? Stressing the value of being God's children is the best starting point. The grace of God, the forgiveness of Christ, and the power and presence of the Holy Spirit are realities that build self-worth in Christians. Beyond that concept being preached, taught, sung, and prayed, what else can be done? There are at least five ways in which a sense of self-esteem can be nurtured in the church.

1. *Develop an edifying climate.* One of the marks of the New Testament Church was the love and concern members had for one another. It was a contagious spirit of caring summed up by the word *edify.* To edify means to build up someone. Sometimes it requires words and sometimes deeds of kindness. Frequently, it includes a pat on the back, a handshake, a squeeze on the shoulder, or a hug.

Developing a climate of edification is not hard in a congregation where members are regularly involved in God's Word. Where this is not the case, the Bible is the place to begin. When the congregation is tuned into God's Word, the spirit of edification catches on like fire. A core of people can be trained to be sensitive and aware of opportunities to edify. People need to look for ways to genuinely compliment or strengthen another person. A sense of positive reinforcement is appreciated by anyone. Corporately, a climate of positive edification fills the air.

The greatest New Testament pattern for edification is the use of spiritual gifts. Paul describes this in Ephesians 4. People aren't jealous of one another because each has a gift (or gifts) from God. There is no sense of failure because every person has at least one gift. When people use their gifts, the end result is love. People become a team and work together under the leadership of Christ.

2. *Find strengths/remove roadblocks.* The second way to build a positive image in the rural church is to concentrate on the strengths. What does this church do best? Every church has unique strengths. Perhaps it has a good choir or a strong Sunday School. It may be known throughout the area for its friendliness. Whatever it is, it should be a point of emphasis for attitude building and developing a sense of corporate self-worth.

Some pastors spend most of their pulpit time talking about the ills of the church. That's a great way to repel visitors. In their day-to-day ministry, some preachers spend much time extinguishing fires and mending fences. Their time could be spent better by taking away the matches and building relationships.

People are attracted to pastors and lay leaders who conduct a positive ministry. The average person likes to be affirmed. Much of the world in which they live is full of hurt and despair, but an affirming congregation draws people. Its contagious infection is caught by visitors. This is one reason a greeter serves an important role in the church. Visitors learn they are welcome. A smile and a handshake is an affirmation. If the greeter's ministry is complemented by a genuinely friendly congregation, this is especially effective. In such churches the affirmation is extended to the parking lot. Sometimes a greeter will meet people at their cars. Some churches even provide guest parking close to the main entrance.

The devil provides many roadblocks to a positive spirit in a church. One of the worst is gossip. Churches that want to maintain a positive image need to deal with this serious problem. The pastor can't do it. Most people do not gossip to him. The leaders of the church need to be models. Christians do not realize the extent to which they are destroying their church when they gossip. People work hard, contribute, and pay for their church, only to dismantle it by casual and idle gossip.

On the other hand, positive, sincere conversations about a person get back to him in a reinforcing way. This is also true when people build up their pastor. Positive reinforcement helps develop a pastor's healthy self-image. The pastor's self-image will reflect on the church. When people genuinely build up the pastor, they remove roadblocks of discouragement.

3. *Give positive motivation.* The pastor pounded the pulpit as his face became red. "The Lord commands us to witness. If you are a Christian, you must be obedient to the Great Commission. Yet, how many of you have ever won one person to Jesus Christ?" This pastor accomplished one major task—he created guilt.

The problem with motivating by guilt or out of a sense of duty is that it doesn't work in a voluntary association like the church. People will not continue going to church if they go home feeling bad about themselves. There is need for the law, but the law does not motivate. It is the gospel that draws people like a magnet into the service of the church.

People are motivated by positive expectations. The young person who is constantly told by his parents that he is a good baseball player will work to achieve that expectation. This is called self-fulfilling prophecy. How can it work in a positive way in the church?

Let's presume that the pastor wants to motivate people to greet visitors after the worship service. There are several ways to do this. The pastor can suggest, in a positive way, that the people take the opportunity to greet those who are visiting. Or, negatively, the pastor can tell the people that it is their Christian duty, and complain about their lack of friendliness to visitors.

The self-fulfilling prophecy method works better than either of these methods. Here's how it works. During the announcements, Pastor John acknowledges the visitors. "Will our visitors today please raise their hands—we'd just like to see who you are. Thank you. Welcome to our church. We pray that our worship service will be a blessing to you, and we hope you'll come back again. We have a very friendly church. Don't be surprised if many of our members come to you and introduce themselves after the service." The end result is that many of the members will follow through on the expectation of their pastor.

4. *Celebrate victories.* Every church has its defeats. One of the positive aspects of a healthy church is the permission to fail. This is not a technique—it is a climate. The leadership of the church will project the expectation that many strategies for ministry will be tried and that some will fail.

Often churches live in fear of defeat. That fear is the greatest defeat of all. A healthy church will promote a willingness to try, to experiment, to test, and to evaluate. If programs don't measure up—they should be scrapped. The end of the program should not be viewed as a defeat for the church. There should be a willingness to risk and permission to drop any program that does not work.

On the other hand, victories should be celebrated. Anytime a building is finished, a person is baptized, or a program is successfully completed, it should be celebrated. Anytime goals are reached there should be celebration.

In the context of the fellowship group, the people should be encouraged to share what God is doing in their lives. God's victories in the church-at-large can be reported in the bulletin or newsletter. This could include denominational growth, a new church in a neighboring community, or the successful completion of a statewide hunger drive.

Personal testimonies were a part of New Testament church life. People in whom God is working should be encouraged to share with the members of the church. When someone becomes well, a baby is born, or a man finds a job, the church should rejoice and thank God. The hallelujahs of the Scripture are literally God's people saying, "Hurray for God." These celebrations build a positive spirit among God's people. They reinforce that God is in this church, and He is doing many things.

5. *Support possibility thinking.* It cannot be denied that possibility thinking has a significant effect on the church. In every church there are chronic complainers and negative thinkers—it's part of the territory. What can be done with them? First, they

need to be accepted. Second, they need to be loved. They are often people who are unhappy with themselves. Third, they should not serve on any board or committee. This is hard to enforce, but at best they should be discouraged from serving until their attitudes reflect the spirit of Christ. Fourth, they should not be given a chance to speak publicly in church meetings. This, too, is often difficult to enforce. Extra discussion and personal attention before meetings may prepare the negative thinkers somewhat.

Every church is blessed with possibility thinkers. They are people who see a possibility in every problem. If one door is shut, they look for another to open. They know that God's people can't lose, and that spirit of victory sets the tone in all they do. These people should be given many opportunities to express their positive views before the church. Their attitudes can leaven the church and bring a positive, corporate self-image.

Philosophy of Ministry

Every church has a philosophy of ministry that reflects the corporate personality of the church. It is the answer to the question, "What makes this church unique?" It is reflected in how the members explain this church to their new neighbors. It is that which distinguishes the church from other congregations in the community. The rural church should have a philosophy of ministry that reflects the rural orientation of the people of that church.

The philosophy of ministry of the church should be written. That way it can be shared and discussed. It can point prospective members to that which makes the church unique. It can also be used as a statement to the community.

A philosophy of ministry should express the positive self-image of the Body of Christ. The church trusts in the promises of God. It lives by the power of God. It celebrates in the presence of God. That reality of God working among His people draws people to himself, and they *grow up*. It connects people in supernatural love to one another, and they *grow together.* God's activity among His people causes them to be freed from the bondage of sin and released to share that precious good news, and the church *grows out.* As God works in the growing church, the people of God see opportunities to start churches in other areas, and the church can *grow more.* This is a positive outreach philosophy of ministry for the church that seeks to be part of the exciting challenge of fulfilling the Lord's Great Commission.

5

Health and Vitality
in the Rural Church

A negative self-image affects the health and vitality of a church. One of the major contributing factors to the dying rural church is that members believe themselves to be part of a dying church.

Glenwood Chapel is a case in point. The church was dying. But why? The potential for life was all around it, but the death of the church was all the people would talk about. They had become preoccupied with the demise of their congregation. Their attitudes would eventually kill them.

The pastor described what he did to shock some reality into the people. One day he rented a casket from the local funeral home. On Sunday he placed the casket in the front of the church. He publicized this service very well, and the sanctuary was packed with people. He preached on the death of Glenwood Chapel. Then at the end of the service, he asked the people to come forward to see the remains of their dead church.

As the people filed up to look into the casket, each discovered that the pastor had placed a large mirror inside. They discovered something about their church and themselves. Today, that church is alive and growing—15 years later.

A Healthy Rural Church

The health of a rural church depends upon more than people's attitudes. When diagnosing health in the rural church, you have to ask, "According to what standards?"

Usually church members connect health to growth. If a church is healthy, it will be growing. This is true when we consider the types of growth mentioned at the end of the last chapter. There are four types of growth, and every rural church can and should see results in two or three of these areas.

1. *Growing up.* This is internal growth. A healthy church is composed of people who are maturing in the Lord. There is a renewed emphasis on Bible study and prayer. In many rural churches, people are breaking away from the old (but not so biblical) idea that only the pastor can lead a Bible study. Laypeople are growing as they study God's Word individually and in groups.

The keys to developing a church with regular Bible studies are priorities, attitudes, and commitment. Bible study must be considered a priority by the pastor and the leaders of the congregation. It must be encouraged constantly. It should become a priority in the church's life-style and be emphasized all year, year after year.

A second key to developing Bible studies in the rural church is attitudes. "Look," explained Ralph, "I only went through the eighth grade. After that my dad needed me on the farm. I'm afraid to get with a group of other people and study the Bible. I don't read so well . . ." Ralph finds the idea of Bible study uncomfortable because it could be embarrassing. The church that wants to develop strong Bible studies must encourage an attitude of acceptance among those involved.

The third key is commitment. People must be committed to the others in their Bible study group. In the rural community where relationships are often well-cemented together, this commitment is an extension of rural life.

Good Bible study groups should number from about 8 to 12 people. They can meet as often as they wish, with a minimum of one meeting each month. Each group can set the day and time that best suits their schedules. In the agricultural life-style, scheduling will take into account the seasons, the crops, the cattle, the chores, and many other aspects of rural life.

Each meeting of the Bible study group will provide time to study God's Word and the opportunity to discuss the price of wheat, the weather, or the swimming pool John and Sally just installed alongside their pole barn.

Every rural church can and should experience internal growth. It is the beginning of all other growth, for churches don't grow unless people grow, and people don't grow unless they study God's Word. Bible study is an important part of the health of every Christian.

2. *Growing together.* Fellowship was central and natural in the rural church of the past. Extended families and longtime neighbors would drive their buggies to church and afterward spend the entire day together until evening chores. After chores they might return for evening worship. The church was *the* local meeting place for fellowship.

With the introduction of the automobile, rural neighbors became more isolated from one another. When two buggies passed on the dirt road, neighbors stopped and talked. All that is left of that slower-paced life is the blast of the horn or a quick wave as cars pass each other on the tarred country road.

Fellowship no longer automatically happens in most rural churches. This is especially true in churches of 200 or more worshipers. As a church gets larger, people can't remember each other's first names. As the agricultural world is more and more mechanized, people don't depend on each other. As various modes of entertainment continue to invade the number of discretionary hours available to each member of the family, get-togethers with friends, relatives, and neighbors diminish. Fellowship gatherings need to be scheduled and planned, even in the rural church.

Fellowship is an integral part of a healthy church. It is essential if a church is to grow because new people need the glue of fellowship if they are going to stay. Without it they will find their way out the back door.

Every rural church can have a healthy pattern of growth when it comes to growing up and growing together. However, the potential for growing larger may be limited in many rural churches.

3. *Growing out.* This type of growth means that more people are joining the church. Attendance at worship grows because the church is reaching out to its area.

In many rural churches this is more possible than most members think. In most counties (or parishes in the Southern United States), only 50 percent of the population will say they belong to a church. Of those 50 percent, many say they belong but can't tell you the name of the present minister. Of those who know the minister's name, there are many who attend rarely.

Surveys, canvasses, and random visiting are ways of educating people to the fact that many of their rural neighbors do not attend church. Most people are astonished by the openness and receptivity of the unchurched population once they start calling on them. It is a learning experience rural church members ought to consider.

Why don't people in rural areas go to church? In studying thousands of people, we've discovered three answers to that question. People say they don't go to church because no one has ever invited them. They also say that the churches they have visited have not been friendly. (What they mean is that the people weren't friendly to them, as visitors.) The third answer people give is that they don't go to church because the sermons are boring.

Sensitizing churchgoers to become experts on the unchurched helps them have eyes wide open to growth. But what about attitudes toward the lost?

This is the second half of the outreach challenge for the rural church. What are the attitudes of the people toward the unchurched? Do they take the Great Commission seriously?

Do they consider it their task, the pastor's, or someone else's? What do they see as the main purpose for Jesus Christ coming to this earth? Did He come to seek and save the lost? Did He die on the Cross primarily that sinners may have forgiveness? When He said, "As the Father sent me, so I send you" (John 20:21, TEV), was He talking to the disciples of His day only, or are those words meant for disciples of all time? What, then, is the top priority for Christians in the church today?

Throughout history, when the Christian church had an understanding of who and what it was and what its priorities were, it has grown. When a proper, biblical self-identity is established among Christian people, they will want to reach out to the unchurched. When that happens, many of the nongrowth excuses in rural churches will fade.

There are, however, some situations where the rural church cannot experience numerical growth. Perhaps the population surrounding the congregation is churched. Perhaps the population is dwindling, and the church is running out of people. In this instance the church cannot and should not be expected to grow through outreach, but it can experience spiritual growth and fellowship growth. It may be able to use its energies to start a church in another area. This is the fourth kind of growth. It is an option that is open to almost every rural church.

4. *Growing more.* This is commonly called church extension or church planting. It happens when one church starts another church. Today there are thousands of rural areas without a church on the North American continent. There are tens of thousands of rural areas with only one or two churches. Since not every church appeals to every prospective Christian, many more churches are needed in the world today. Some will be liturgical; some will be informal. Some will speak Spanish; others English; some German. Some appeal to youth; others will be for retirement-aged people. Each will attract people like themselves.

Many rural churches are 20 or 30 minutes by car from areas that do not have a church of their denomination or expression of worship life. These areas represent opportunities for church planting.

In the United States, the average unchurched person will travel no more than 12 to 15 minutes to attend a church. There are exceptions to this because there are exceptional churches and pastors that draw people great distances. However, the average church's ministry area can be defined by drawing a boundary that represents 12 to 15 minutes traveling time from the church. In the rural area this can be expanded to 20 minutes because people are accustomed to traveling longer distances.

On this basis, many rural churches can consider the possibilities for planting a church. If every rural church did this, the impact would be phenomenal in thousands of towns in North America. Those churches who feel they can't afford it make two common mistakes. The first is called the edifice complex. They think that to begin a church they have to buy land and build a building. But many churches can start in homes or borrowed facilities. The second big mistake is that they think the new church must have a fully trained, ordained minister to start. Many new churches start through the efforts of neighboring pastors. Others are started by trained lay leaders under the direction of another pastor. Still others come into being through the efforts of bivocational workers—those who are trained to a degree but earn most of their income through a secular means of employment. With these various options for growth, every healthy rural church can experience growth in some way.

Removing Rural Roadblocks to Health

What about an unhealthy church? Health is the absence of disease. There are several diseases that strike the rural church. These diseases can be considered roadblocks to the health of the church.

There are at least six roadblocks to health in the rural church. Discovering them, diagnosing them, and removing them are the ways in which rural churches can foster health.

1. _Can the word "can't."_ Pessimism and defeat in many rural churches cripple what can be accomplished through faith. Reality awareness is important. The recognition of certain limitations is essential. However, the church in the rural setting is in need of encouragement and challenge. Hebrews 11 is the story of several rural people who did some phenomenal things because they released their fears and let God work through them.

It's not a matter of weak faith among agriculturally oriented people. These people see the miracle of birth, life, growth, and harvest much more clearly than people in urban areas. Why is it, then, that people in rural churches are hesitant to go forward boldly? The problem may not be their lack of faith in God but their lack of faith in themselves.

This, too, seems puzzling because of the rugged individualism found among rural people. But a strange phenomenon seems to take place. Many of these risk-taking, adventurous people change hats mentally when they enter the world of their church life. Why? Perhaps it goes back to being small. It may have something to do with society's idea that the city is where "the action is" and rural is "out there in the middle of nowhere." Or it may be tied to a denomination's subtle indifference to the rural church or the attitudes of pastors, as was discussed previously.

Whatever the cause, it can be overcome by positive, aggressive, and challenging leadership. More and more rural churches, led by dynamic pastors, are accomplishing great things in what could be called turnaround ministries.

Bethlehem Church is an example. The congregation was unable to attract a pastor for several years. The defeated attitude of the people was reflected by the white frame building that badly needed a paint job. Landscaping and lawn care had been neglected.

Pastor Bachman arrived fresh out of seminary. He was a second-career pastor, having spent 10 years as an accountant. He was excited about his call to this little parish. He arrived with a positive attitude. His philosophy was: God has sent me to this group of people, growth is possible, and God can do anything. This pastor's excitement was a breath of fresh air for the 144-year-old parish. Before long he felt comfortable to challenge the people to fix up the church. As they were investigating the cost of paint, someone suggested vinyl siding. The cost would be about the same as half of last year's budget. In the middle of the skeptic's cries of "It can't be done," they raised the money, and the church was sided. Soon afterward one of the members volunteered to provide new landscaping.

The congregation began to grow. Within two years, the people were pressed for room for Sunday School classes. They were challenged to build. As they raised $125,000 for their building project, the vinyl siding project of only two years before seemed insignificant. Rural churches have potential for monumental accomplishments if the leadership will only work to can the word *can't*.

2. *Treat your money like manure.* Someone has said: "Money is like manure: it's really not much good unless it is spread around." Lack of finances is a stranglehold that blocks health in the rural church.

Many rural churches are shackled by what they perceive to be insufficient funds. Sometimes this is a matter of dwindling membership reflected by a shrinking population. This financial situation requires creative management, but its causes are beyond the control of the church. In other rural churches, the financial stranglehold is because of a lack of vision and challenge. It requires good stewardship education and a keen understanding of the rural economy to change the congregation's attitudes about finances.

3. *Look over the crops.* Many rural churches are surrounded by a great harvest of unchurched people, but they don't see them. They see them as neighbors, relatives, veterinarians, grocers, the fuel man, the implement dealer, and the schoolteacher—but they don't see them as prospects.

The success of surveys, canvasses, evangelism calls, and census studies is in direct proportion to the sensitivity of Christians toward the fields that are "white unto harvest." Are they looking? Do they care? Is it a priority?

Jim is a good example of failure to recognize the harvest. He confessed, "You know, I've been a Chrsitian all my life. I grew up in the church, went to Sunday School, and read the Bible a lot. I read those sections about making disciples and preaching the gospel to the whole world, but it never really sunk in. I mean, it never became personal. I used to think of the Lord's harvest the way a lot of city folks think of these oats here. They think of the crops 'out there' somewhere. I used to think that way about mission work. It was 'out there.' Well it is—but it's here too.

"When the new pastor came, he emphasized it more. He talked a lot about church growth. He helped us see that every day we come into contact with people who don't go to church. I can't believe the number of people I know who don't know Christ personally. I just never realized.

"One day the pastor asked me to read a book. I told him I didn't read much, but he said that was no problem. He gave me a set of cassette tapes all about church growth. I have a cassette player in the cab of my combine and I listened to them all the way through twice. You know, I really *do* see things differently!"

Now Jim sees the crops—the Lord's harvest fields. Furthermore, he sees them as his responsibility. Church growth teachers call that "church growth eyes." It is Great Commission vision that is being caught by tens of thousands of people. It is making a difference in the health and growth of churches.

If the rural church desires a healthy vision, the members need to discuss the harvest fields of people-groups that can be reached with the gospel. Are they people like the people of the church? Can they be reached best by inviting them to our church? Should we start another service on a Saturday evening that would be more appealing to a certain group in our area? Should we start a different type or style of service? Should we plant a church? As the members of the church look at their ministry area with sensitivity, they begin to develop strategies for each mission field—each people-group. They realize that even in rural areas not every crop is the same. It's easy for people in agriculture to understand that the harvest method has to match the crop if you want a good harvest.

4. *Cultivate: remove the weeds that choke.* One of the roadblocks to health that infects all churches is the nongrowth weeds that crop up in the growth path of a visitor. It can be a severe problem in rural churches where: (*a*) the members aren't accustomed to many visitors; (*b*) the membership consists of many close-knit families; or (*c*) the church is small enough that everyone knows everyone else.

The weeds show up in subtle ways. No visitor parking is one weed that is common. Another is that the sign in front of the church doesn't give the times of services. Many churches have a worship service full of weeds. These are unintelligible "in" words and expressions that leave the visitors with the idea that they weren't expected and aren't really wanted. In many churches the visitor can't find the rest rooms without asking for directions. This is a dead giveaway that the church doesn't expect visitors.

If visitors find a receptive church, what are the chances they will join? Here is another opportunity to cultivate. Cultivation in the fields or the garden isn't just for weeds. It provides air in the soil and allows rain to get to the roots of young plants. Young Christians, like young plants, need care if they are to bear fruit.

This type of cultivation can be called nurture. The church that wants the young Christian to grow like a vine connected to the branch of Christ must take care to see that young Christian gets fed. The Christian's food is the Word of God.

The healthy church will provide instruction opportunities to cultivate new Christians and those seeking a church home. Many churches begin by prompt follow-up on visitors, sending them a letter or a postcard. This is followed by a visit. One of the most productive calls is a visit to the home of people soon after they have visited. This call is best made by laypeople. Some unchurched people would look upon a pastor as one who is there because it's his job. A nonthreatening, friendly call may be more helpful at first. The pastor can call later if visitors express continued interest.

If people decide to join a church, will they stay? Will they feel they are a part of the church? Will they feel the church is their own? This aspect of cultivation is called assimilation. If it doesn't happen, new members may go out the back door and become inactives.

Research shows that if people are to become assimilated into a church, at least three things need to happen. First, they need to be involved in a task or assume a role in the church. This can be an elected position or any job that needs to be done, including ushering, being a nursery attendant, or helping on a cleanup campaign. Second, they need to be involved in a small group where their fellowship needs are met. This should be a structured group that intentionally meets at least once each month. It can be a home Bible study group, a couples' club, a youth group, or a ladies' society. Finally, they need to become good friends with at least seven other people in the church.

5. *Consider the miracle of the corncob.* One corn kernel, planted and nurtured, cultivated and grown to maturity, will often produce two ears of corn. These ears of corn can contain 200 or more kernels. This is the beauty of God's creation, the miracle of multiplication. One old Chinese proverb speaks of this concept in a different way: "You can count the number of seeds in an apple, but you can't count the number of apples in a seed."

God's kingdom is designed to expand and grow by multiplication. Some people have said, "Let the pastor do it." In many churches the pastor has implied, "Only a clergyman can do it and do it right." The Bible talks about the ministry belonging to every Christian. Scripture uses the image of a priesthood of all believers.

Churches grow better if the pastor is a leader who teaches and trains people to do the work of ministry. The concept of multiplication is easy to understand. The laypeople of a small church can do more ministry in their spare time than the pastor can working full time. If the pastor spends time and energy training others for the work of ministry, then there is multiplication.

More and more rural churches are leading people to be involved and activated for meaningful ministry. The key is in the goal of evangelism. Is the goal to make church members or to make disciples? The Scriptures indicate that people are to become disciples. They are to grow in the faith, follow Jesus, be lifelong learners of His way, and take up their crosses to do the ministry to which He has called them.

This is especially helpful for the health and growth of a congregation because laypeople have day-to-day contact with the world. Most of the contacts pastors have are with those who are already Christians and members of churches. Laypeople can witness, serve, and help their neighbors in natural ways that the professional pastor can't. There is no doubt that this biblical method of multiplication is the key to the successful harvest. It's a fact of God's creation. Without multiplication, where would the corn crop be?

6. *Prime the pump.* One of the basic roadblocks in many rural churches is that people are not enthused about growth. The challenge that faces the pastor and leadership of such a church is to prime the pump and build enthusiasm. The word *enthusiasm* literally means "in God." People who are in Christ are excited and enthused—they have a passion for the lost. Right?

Wrong! The difficulty does not lie in the area of commitment and faith or lack of spirituality. Often the problem is due to lack of education and motivation. There is more. Many rural churches are single-cell fellowships. While this description is usually reserved for small churches, it can include larger church-es. A church is single-cell when it: (a) meets in one group; and (b) everyone knows and talks to almost everyone else. Due to the family relationships in many rural settings, the tendency to perpetuate the single-cell church is strong.

What does the single-cell mind-set do to retard growth? Most of the people in this type of church have seen growth only by biological additions. Families in the congregation have children and these children are brought up in the church. Meanwhile, the members of the church want to maintain an atmosphere in which everyone can know everyone else. There is a subconscious aversion to growth, which subtly repels newcomers.

Twelve Ways to Prime the Pump

The roadblocks that dampen enthusiasm are the single-cell factor, lack of education, and low motivation. There are at least 12 ways to prime the pump. The first 2 are designed to break the single-cell factor. The next 5 are for educating the members toward growth possibilities. The last 5 are directed toward the motivation task. Together, these actions can build enthusiasm and kindle excitement for growth in the rural congregation.

1. *Break the single cell by developing two worship services.* This is helpful if the second service has a different *style* of worship. This method plants another church within the church.

2. *Develop other groups in the congregation.* These groups can take the form of another men's club or ladies' group or choir. It may be a Bible study group that meets for fellowship and study of God's Word. If the single-cell structure is broken in a congregation, the fellowship needs of members must be met in other ways. As this is accomplished, people recognize that changing from a single cell to a multi-cell congregation is not a problem. Their fellowship needs are met. People begin to look at their church with an openness to growth. But this doesn't prime the pump of enthusiasm. It sets the stage. Now members need to be educated and motivated.

3. *Study the tone of Scripture.* Through Bible study, people can be led to see the Lord's passion and priority for the lost. Not

only is this priority located in the Great Commission of Matthew 28, but it is a persistent theme throughout Scripture.

The Lord wants the idea of expansion and growth to be a part of the way of life for the Christian church. This is true of every church, even the church that is located in the rural area. It is God's will that the church find the lost and bring them into God's kingdom.

Sometimes in rural areas, it seems like everyone already belongs to a church. In some cases that may be true, but it would be very rare that every single person in an expanded area around the church would already be a Christian. There are always some that need to be reached with the gospel.

Further, it is important to see that growth in maturity and understanding of Jesus Christ is an important part of the overall tone of Scripture. We are to "grow in the grace and knowledge of our Lord and Savior Jesus Christ" (2 Pet. 3:18, TEV). The Bible is the key to opening eyes to see God's will. It helps us recognize the mission of the church.

Karen and Walt have been members of the congregation at Hale's Corner all their lives. But when the new pastor came, they were not involved in any Bible study and attended church irregularly. Pastor Daly visited their home. He informed them he had been praying for them and had made a special visit to invite them to join an adult Bible class.

That was all it took. Walt and Karen appreciated the personal invitation. They had not had visitors from the church for a long time, except when it was time to raise pledges for the next year's budget. They responded and started attending the Bible class. They soon realized that they, as Christians, needed to continue to grow. They also recognized that there were others in the community who, although they had loose ties to the church, did not attend church regularly. Studying the tone and nature of Scripture helped them to see that the church is supposed to be a vital, growing entity.

4. *Make a graph of the past growth or decline of the congregation.* It is not unusual in a congregation, whether it be a rural or city church, to find a lack of accurate records. There are a num-

ber of ways to gather statistics. First of all, if you have statistics for some years but not for others, guesstimate the time in between. Another way to deal with lack of information is by interviewing some of the members of the congregation who have been active in past years. They can help make a good guesstimate for any particular year. In either case, do the best you can, and gather the information for each year. You may want to gather information for membership, attendance in worship, and attendance in Sunday School and adult Bible class.

Then plot out the membership on a graph. It may seem like a big job to gather information and plot it on a graph, but it is a lot easier than calibrating machinery for proper herbicide spray. If several people in the congregation can be involved in this project, it is not only less work but also a learning exercise for everyone involved.

Once you have developed the graph, put it on a bulletin board, show it in worship, or put a copy of it in the bulletin. Help people see a picture of your church's growth.

A graph shows the health and vitality of a congregation over a period of time. It shows where the congregation is growing, declining, expanding, or dying. It is a picture of your congregation's growth. It is a snapshot of history. It will help people become aware of the health and vitality of your church.

5. *Look at the facts.* Begin to ask the question of how many people are unchurched in your area. There are companies that gather this information by county, using census data. They report all the churches in the area, and they provide information on how many people go to church and what percentage of the county is churched and unchurched. They can tell how many people belong to each denomination.

While this information can be expensive to gain for the entire county, many agencies have this information available for the work that they do. For example, the Church Growth Center in Corunna, Ind., where I work, has this information and uses it constantly in the consultation ministry. For a small charge, most agencies will provide this information for your church. Your own denomination may have some of this information as well.

Another way to get a handle on the people of your area is to discover how many of them are known by people of your church. To do this, you can use a sociogram. Use a piece of 8½" x 11" paper with a circle in the middle. In the circle is a horizontal line for the person's name. Ask the people in your congregation to list in the upper right corner of the sociogram all the people they know who are unchurched and who are friends. Second, in the upper left corner ask them to list all the people they know who are unchurched who are relatives. In the lower left corner ask them to list all the people they would consider to be neighbors who are unchurched. In the lower right corner ask them to list all the people who are contacts at work or school and are unchurched. You may want to define the geographical area that is the ministry area of your church. Take a map and put a pin on your church location. Then outline an area around your church that is no farther than 12 to 20 minutes traveling distance from your church. This will not be a circle, but would follow the main roads and traffic patterns that people use to get to your church.

Pastor Wagner followed this example at his rural church in northeastern Ohio. Pastor Wagner's church had an average of 226 people in worship. Of those people, 80 percent agreed to participate in this activity. They discovered 1,238 unchurched people who lived within 20 minutes of their congregation. These people were friends, relatives, neighbors, or contacts at work or school.

This gathering of the facts helped Pastor Wagner see how many unchurched people were in the area. It also helped the people of the congregation discover how many unchurched people they knew collectively.

Rev. Donna Krale of Kelly's Hollow Church in rural Vermont heard about what Pastor Wagner had done and decided to move the effort one step further. She went to the nearest city and hired an agency with a word processing computer and printing facility. She asked them to develop a mailing list from the names and the addresses that her members compiled of their unchurched friends, relatives, neighbors, and people with whom they worked or went to school.

Every time there was a special event at Kelly's Hollow, Pastor Krale phoned the company and asked them to print a personal letter to all those on the mailing list, inviting them to that upcoming event. Pastor Krale signed every one.

This happened five times a year: at Christmas, Easter, when the youth group had a drama, when a college choir was traveling through the area and sang at the church, and when the church had the annual hog roast. As people in the congregation saw the potential for reaching other people and knew that the congregation was inviting them, they began to personally invite people to come to their church.

When visitors came for one of these special events, they would register their names through various means that the evangelism committee had developed. These ways of registration were different, depending on the event. The evangelism group followed up on these contacts with another letter saying how thankful they were that they came and attended their church and invited them to come back again. Many of them did. Many of those people decided to join Kelly's Hollow. So, the church discovered and reached out to many people, after knowing the facts about their ministry area.

6. *Consider how God might lead your church to grow.* Begin by praying and asking God to direct you according to His will. Include this prayer as a part of your worship service on a regular basis. It should be the prayer of every board and committee as they meet to do ministry within your church.

Ask the people of your congregation to pray personally for their part in the ministry of the church. At the New Haven Community Church in northern Michigan, Pastor Ben Manthe organized the congregation for an all-night prayer vigil. Members of the congregation signed up for a time slot and came into the sanctuary to pray at their appointed time. This prayer vigil was the beginning of great blessings that God showered upon the church. It was also a way in which the people were sensitized to the opportunities that existed for outreach and growth of the church.

As you pray, look at the past performance of your congregation as it appears on graphs. Now consider the future. Asking

God to lead you, choose some goals. Target a goal that you think God is leading your church to accept. Then envision that goal. Believe that you have attained it, as Scripture directs (Matt. 18:19). Begin to develop strategies to attain that goal under God's blessing and with His help.

7. *Firm up and set your goal as a faith projection.* Project the goals that you think God wants you to reach in various areas of your church's life in the next year. Perhaps this will include membership. You may want to deal with worship attendance. Another important area in which to set goals is Bible study. You may want to consider Sunday School attendance or the number of youth involved in the church.

One of the essential steps in this goal-setting process is to develop ownership throughout the congregation. Therefore, as the pastor and key leaders set goals, it is important to process them through the church. Let everybody know that you are praying for the Lord's guidance. Ask them to pray with you. Ask for people's input. When the goals have been set, share them with the congregation and ask them what they think. Be sincere about your desire to receive their input. Then let everyone decide. Take a vote. Let the people have a say in the adoption of these goals.

Once the goals are adopted, communicate them back to the congregation. Tell the congregation over and over the goals they have chosen. Post them in a conspicuous place so that the people can see them regularly and be reminded that God is leading.

8. *Lead the members of your church to appreciate the grace of God given to them.* Celebrate God's goodness and love to you. Have an Eph. 2:8-9 celebration. We are saved by God's grace, not by works. During the celebration, give thanksgiving for all the blessings God has given to individuals. This can be at the Thanksgiving holiday, which is very special in the rural church, or it can be at any other time.

The little Norwegian church of Centerville was founded in 1853. For their celebration they listed all of those who were baptized, married, and buried through the ministries of their church. They estimated how many had heard the gospel over the years, how many sermons had been preached, how many Bible classes had been taught, and how many Sunday School classes had been provided for children. This was not an exercise in patting themselves on the back; this was an opportunity to praise God.

When things go right in the church, celebrate the victories. All too often people tend to concentrate on the negative. Some individuals are notoriously negative. They shouldn't be given the opportunity to set the tone for the congregation.

Too many rural churches have low self-esteem. Sometimes there are good reasons for that. However, the best reason for being positive and excited is boasting about what God can do. Appreciate God's grace. This is an important aspect of having a healthy and vital church.

9. *Practice Jesus' love for others.* Remember the story of Peter asking Jesus, "Lord, if my brother keeps on sinning against me, how many times do I have to forgive him? Seven times?" (Matt. 18:21, TEV). Jesus had a surprise answer for Peter. He told Peter that the kingdom of God is different from the kingdoms of the world. Jesus told him that he should forgive 70 times 7.

Jesus taught us to pray "forgive us our debts [or trespasses], as we forgive our debtors [or those who have trespassed against us]" (Matt. 6:12). In that prayer, we are asking God to forgive us in the same way that we forgive others. It is a statement of a faith, and it is a statement of behavior.

Think about a sore that gets infected. It gathers pus, and it becomes painful. This is what happens to the Body of Christ when people do not forgive one another.

We need to forgive others as God has forgiven us. We need to tell them that God has forgiven them and so do we. The way to forgive is to focus on the Cross. If we cannot forgive each other in the church, how can we share Christ's forgiveness with people out in the world? That is important for a vital church. There are so many people who need to know about Jesus Christ. They are people you know. They are people at the co-op, the feed mill, the hardware store, and the hairdresser. They are people for whom Christ died. They need to hear about forgiveness. The most effective message about the forgiveness of Jesus Christ comes from people who are not only forgiven but forgiving.

10. *We are in partnership with the Lord of the universe.* The Lord has called the church to a unique mission. Oh, the church can duplicate what many other people are doing in life, in social agencies, government agencies, the Boy Scouts, and other groups. It usually duplicates what these other people are doing poorly, however, because it is not really the purpose of the church to be doing those things. But there is something the church can do that no other group can do—tell people about salvation in Jesus Christ.

Think about this: long after the mines run out, the timber is harvested, or the farm is sold, what will last?

The Lord calls us to lay up treasures in heaven. Recent research revealed interesting facts about values in life. People over 90 years old were interviewed and asked if they were to live their lives over again, what they would do differently. One of the most frequent responses was that they would invest more of their time in activities and efforts that would outlast their lives.

Jesus called himself the Vine and said we are the branches (John 15:5). He said that we don't have any life without being connected to Him. There is no chance of bearing fruit without that close relationship to the Vine, Jesus Christ.

The Gardener, the Father, prunes us so that we can produce more fruit. In this section of Scripture, the Lord shows us that we did not choose Him, but He has chosen us to be in partnership with Him, the Lord of the universe. He says that we are to go and produce much fruit. It is not supposed to be ordinary fruit, but fruit that abides, fruit that lasts, fruit that is eternal.

The Great Commission is a commissioning from a King. We are under marching orders. But it is also a great co-mission. Like the co-op, it is a cooperative mission. It is the greatest mission, the greatest adventure, and the greatest work in which people can be involved.

If you raise crops, you know how exciting it is to bring in the harvest. Think of how all of heaven rejoices over one sinner who repents (Luke 15:7). Think of what a party goes on in the Kingdom when one person receives the Lord. This is the greatest adventure known to humankind. A growing, vital, and healthy church has a keen awareness of this partnership with the Lord of the universe.

11. *Celebrate the victories as God gives them to you.* Celebrate God's love for His people. List all the blessings God has given to you in His grace. Celebrate victories. Sometimes, we find false humility in the church. We act as though it is a sin to celebrate when things go well. We fail to honor people who have done a good job. We forget to thank those people who have served faithfully. We spend more time raising the money than we do celebrating once it is raised. We work harder on building the new building than we do celebrating and thanking God when it is completed.

We need to give ourselves permission to boast of what God is doing. We need to take inventory and see how many victories are all around us.

When consulting churches, we seek to affirm and build. When a church calls in a consultant, they are concerned that they will be embarrassed by the problems the consultant exposes. They are afraid that they will be discouraged by difficulties that are underscored by the consultant's presence and his report. We have found that instead of fault-finding, it is more important to be fact-finding. We do not talk about problems: we talk about challenges. We recognize that problems are often opportunities in disguise. We affirm and build. We accentuate the strengths of the congregation and ask, "How can the congregation build on these strengths?" This is an important part of leadership in the healthy and vital church: helping people learn the life-style of "affirm and build." It is so much more productive than nit-picking.

12. *Make growth your priority.* How do you know a priority when you see it? Priorities are those things that take first place over other things. You can identify priorities by the amount of time, energy, and money spent on certain issues.

Another way of identifying time use and priorities is to look at how the pastor uses time. What are the pastor's priorities? How do the groups in your church spend their energy?

At the Browncastle Church, the ladies' group has energetic

and hard workers. They really get enthused about fund-raisers, especially the annual bazaar. However, when it comes to personal Bible study, developing fellowship for new members in the church, or reaching out to the community, the ladies' group just cannot get enthused. In the same church, the men's group gets involved in horseshoe tournaments, dart ball, or the annual fishing trip. However, when it comes to giving a helping hand to those in need, or canvassing the area, it is hard to get anyone to participate. The youth group is really excited when they get together for a pizza party. But a Bible study? That is another story.

What is the problem? It is just that the people have their priorities in the wrong places.

What does your budget say? How money is spent is a great way to identify the priorities of the church. If you wanted to raise money for an evangelist, could you do it? Would it be easier if the same amount of money was needed to fix the roof?

Money is important because of what it represents. It represents our values, and it represents our crystallized sweat. It is personal. It is important. How we spend it in the church is a strong reflection of our priorities.

Healthy churches reflect Jesus looking at the crowds, looking at the mission, looking at the vision for world evangelization. They are involved in outreach growth and have an eye to the harvest.

6

The Rural Pastor

*T*he air in the seminary chapel was filled with expectancy. For several years, John had studied diligently for the ministry. His wife, Tris, sacrificed much to help him through the seminary.

Now, all the hours of work, the tens of thousands of pages of reading, the exams, the hours and hours of classroom study, all seemed to fade into a fuzz of history as John and Tris focused on this moment when they should receive their assignment to their very first congregation.

When John and Tris interviewed with the seminary placement director, they had discussed their willingness to serve on the East Coast or the West Coast. But they were numb with shock when it was announced they would be serving a church in Hudson . . . North Dakota. Shock No. 2 came when it was stated that their *other* congregation would be in Agnes, about 37 miles south. And when they consulted an atlas and discovered that both were isolated communities, they were almost devastated.

Sleep evaded them that night as they discussed their future with mixed emotions. John even thought about other churches with a different system for pastors seeking churches. In his own church body, a little-known placement director had just cast his future to North Dakota.

Both John and Tris had grown up in Baltimore. They enjoyed the many cultural opportunties of the large city. This would be quite a drastic change for them.

They reviewed the information and found that the church at Hudson averaged 50 people in worship. That seemed small until they read further and discovered that Agnes was even smaller. Neither could afford a full-time minister and had a "yoked" ministry for the last three decades. There was no indication whether the churches were growing or declining; nothing about the average age of the membership. Farming and ranching were noted as the primary life-styles of the region.

After finally falling asleep about 3 A.M., they were jolted awake when the telephone rang at 8:00. For the caller, the day was already four hours old. Don had just finished breakfast. As head deacon, it was his job to call the new seminary graduate who had been assigned to his church at Hudson. John thought it was much too early for a Saturday morning call. It was only a fleeting thought, but it was a thought that he would have many times later as his life-style changed over the coming months.

"That was Don Phillips," said John. "He seemed like a nice guy. He said he was into ranching and that they were really happy to have a pastor, finally."

"Anything else?" asked Tris.

"Yeah, he asked if I owned a pair of cowboy boots!" replied John.

John did not have a pair of cowboy boots, nor had he ever dreamed that he would be pastoring in a rural area. Certainly, he had never given any thought to having *two* churches. As the pastor of two rural churches, he was facing some unique experiences.

Church analysts and consultants agree that the recognized key ingredient to a healthy and vital church is the pastor. Many books have been written about the pastor as a key strength to a vital church or a serious detriment to the congregation's health and growth. Leadership revolves around the pastor.

Pastors have tremendous power in the congregation. They can either provide a strength and focus for a positive future, or they can be the bottleneck of progress. This happens in at least four ways.

1. *Instigate or stagnate?* Pastoral leadership can instigate new programs and new ideas. Energetic pastors can constantly be developing new avenues of ministry within the congregation, to the congregation, or through the congregation to the surrounding area. Or pastoral leadership can cause stagnation within a con-

gregation. Often the people will assume the attitude and fervor of the pastor. If the pastor is lazy, or if the pastor is maintenance-oriented, the congregation could easily fall into the same life-style.

"Remember Pastor Gary?" Fred asked Brent as they paused to refuel the tractor.

"I sure do," said Brent. "He was a real go-getter!"

"Yes, I really liked Gary," replied Fred. "He started so many new things. He was an energetic man. Our church was really humming at that time. I like Pastor Larry all right," he reflected on their present pastor, "but he doesn't seem to have that drive that Gary had, you know what I mean?"

Brent nodded. He knew exactly what Fred meant. It wasn't something the congregation aggressively complained about. It's just that the pace of life and the excitement of ministry was somehow dampened under the present pastor's leadership. Pastor Gary instigated. Pastor Larry held the status quo. The congregation, however, stagnated.

2. *Initiate or frustrate?* Pastoral leadership can initiate new ideas and inspire new vision in the people. On the other hand, it can frustrate the initiative of key leaders who are excited and want to serve.

Depending on the attitude and perspective of ministry, a pastor can initiate and ignite spiritual fires among individuals and boards to release them for ministry. The pastor can introduce new ideas, suggestions, and challenges. The pastor can stretch people's horizons and worldviews to ministry and opportunities for mission at home and beyond.

But sometimes, pastoral leadership doesn't initiate, it frustrates. If the pastor is a control-oriented person who feels that he or she must follow the primary task of "keeping everything decently and in good order," it results in a "don't rock the boat" mentality. Furthermore, it is paternalistic. It is leadership that is like an overbearing parent. Such leadership is seen as permission-giving, or more often, permission-denying. It frustrates the very best of lay leadership. In extreme cases, it drives the most energetic and excited members of the church away. In their frustration, they go to serve God someplace else, where their energies will be put to use and their ideas will be appreciated.

3. *Propagate or suffocate?* Pastoral leadership in vital and growing churches multiplies itself. The style for this leadership is to train and empower individuals to do the work of the ministry. The pastoral leader is one who motivates, inspires, and equips people for ministry. This kind of leadership helps individuals find their spiritual gifts and develop those areas of ministry in which God has gifted them.

At the other extreme is the pastor who suffocates. This style of leadership is often based on the assumption that only the pastor can do "real" ministry. It implies that if something is going to be done right, the pastor must do it. This suffocates people who are key leaders and potential leaders within the church. The dominating ministry style of the pastor provides a model for young people who grow up understanding very clearly that the place of the layperson is to "stay, pray, and pay." Young people who are unstable or who have a low self-esteem view the pastor as one who can have power to "keep others in their place." This motivates the next generation of incompetent pastors and perpetuates a leadership style that suffocates churches.

4. *Stimulate or intimidate?* Pastoral leadership can stimulate the growth of the church by encouraging and providing enthusiasm for the congregation. This is particularly important in a rural church where the pastor, to a great degree, needs to be a cheerleader. Many rural churches need encouragement, support, and direction. On the other hand, some pastoral leadership actually intimidates people, quelling their excitement and enthusiasm.

Bill Rauh had been a member of the Coldwater Church for 10 years. He had been particularly active in the church, serving in several key ministries. He was excited when Pastor Jeff was assigned to his church. Jeff was young, so Bill thought he would be open to new ideas. Bill was surprised by Pastor Jeff's reaction when he enthusiastically suggested that the congregation get involved in a life-style evangelism program. Bill was willing to be trained and was eager to begin. Pastor Jeff's voice volume and tone changed noticeably when he told Bill that he wasn't sure about the theological accuracy of such a program, and that he would have to check it out. Further, if Bill wanted to pursue this, he would have to bring it up to the evangelism committee. He hastened to add that Bill should be aware that the congregation had already tried different evangelism programs. Pastor Jeff let Bill know that most of the congregational members were too busy or uninterested in outreach and evangelism. Bill was clearly intimidated.

Pastoral leadership can make or break a congregation. The rural church is particularly fragile. Pastoral leadership is an important part of the entire life and future of the rural church. Much of the way the pastor leads depends on his or her values and attitudes toward the rural church.

"I heard you were assigned to two rural churches in North Dakota," Sam said to John as they bumped into each other in the seminary bookstore. "What did you do wrong to deserve that?" he joked. John didn't think it was funny, but he had to admit the same thought had crossed his mind.

Our research shows that a large number of seminary students view the rural church with inaccurate assumptions. These assumptions are not in the best interests of the pastor or the rural church. Nevertheless, they exist and they shape the values the pastor has when going to the rural congregation. These assumptions are interwoven and interrelated. There are at least six of them.

1. *Rural is less valuable, less exciting, less important than suburban, small town, or urban.* This assumption is usually based on lack of experience or ignorance about the rural church. Such an assumption will cause the pastor to enter the rural setting with lowered expectations. Many rural churches are beehives of activities and excitement. Excellent ministry takes place in the rural setting. God has no bias against rural settings. Jesus was from Nazareth.

Rural ministry is valuable because it is ministry to people for whom Christ died. These are real people with real problems, and some exciting things take place in their lives.

2. *No long-term growth is possible.* From a human perspec-

tive this may be the case for some rural churches. In many rural places, there is an out-migration of people toward suburbs and cities. However, it is not universally true. There are many rural areas that are growing and expanding.

In rural areas where population growth is being experienced, the changes that are occurring are the most dramatic in more than 100 years, if ever. Some rural churches are found on the cutting edge of a burgeoning metroplex. Other rural churches are being changed by the influx of people seeking recreational activities. Harbor Beacon Church at Jamesville is an example of this. When snowmobiling became popular in the 1960s, the Park Service developed snowmobile trails throughout the region. People coming to snowmobile discovered the beautiful landscape of the area. Shops and businesses sprang up to accommodate the winter visitors. This brought population growth to the area, bringing even more shops and services. People began to retire from areas in southern Michigan and relocate in Jamesville or nearby. Many would live in the area seven months of the year and spend five months at a winter residence in Arizona or Florida. For Harbor Beacon Church, this is a rural setting with tremendous long-term growth possiblities.

3. *Temporary tenure is the rule.* Many pastors leave seminary for rural ministries with the mind-set that the rural church will be a two- or three-year stepping-stone to something "better." Consequently, many rural churches have a revolving pulpit as young pastors come and go. Further, those churches never really get involved in long-range planning because they realize that another pastor will come along soon. While God may indeed move pastors to other settings, it is detrimental for the pastor to enter the rural church feeling that this is only temporary. Such a mind-set will discourage deep relationships, long-term planning, and in-depth programming. The assumption of temporary ministry actually becomes a self-fulfilling prophecy.

4. *Big is better.* When two seminarians receive their assignments, one to a small, rural church and the other to be an assistant pastor in a church of over 400, there is a subtle tendency to compare and believe that big is better. While it may sound un-

usual coming from a representative of the Church Growth Movement, it is important to recognize that church growth teaches that "effectively making disciples" is better, not necessarily that "big" is better. Effectively administering the Great Commission is what is important. Sometimes, God grows His Church effectively by planting many new, small, growing churches rather than through one large, maintenance-oriented church.

There are some qualities in the smaller church that the big church does not have. If a pastor is assigned to a small, rural church, there are many strengths the pastor might expect to encounter. These may include a larger per capita involvement ratio, more fellowship, easier communication, stronger relationships, and an easier structure for change.

The other part of the assumption is that rural is necessarily small. This is not the case either. Sometimes rural churches are small. Sometimes they can be large.

5. *Rural is a nice place to retire.* Many pastors see the rural church as a church suitable for the end of the pastoral vocation. It is often viewed as a place to wind down or where older pastors are put out to pasture. This assumption is also a mistaken one. The rural setting can be a marvelous place to raise children. Hunting, fishing, hiking, the garden behind the parsonage, the pet goat, the three cats, the hay rides, the hog roast, the 4-H chapter, and the county fair are only a few of the unique environmental factors that might be readily available to the children of the rural pastor. Of course, the rural pastor would want to make trips to the big city with the children to see that they are exposed to museums, symphonies, ethnic restaurants, multicultural neighborhoods, major league sporting events, and rides in a 25-story elevator. However, this is no different from the urban pastor who would want to expose his children to the farm animals at the petting zoo.

The rural setting can be a wonderful place for the pastor to retire. It can also be an excellent place for the pastor to raise a family.

6. *Rural ministry is for the pastor who can't cut it elsewhere.* This is also the assumption that underlined the comment made to John at the bookstore.

"I think we missed it and have crossed over into Canada," mused John as he and Tris traveled over a large hill.

"No," said Tris, "the North Dakota border, according to this map, ought to be just a few miles up ahead."

John and Tris were about to enter totally new territory. The new territory wasn't just North Dakota or the pastoral ministry—something for which they had been training for several years. The new territory was a rural culture. They didn't know it, but they were going to feel like strangers at first. They were going to learn some new language and new language patterns. They were going to experience a different kind of life-style and eat some new kinds of food. They were going to adjust their timetable for daily living. John and Tris were about to enter the agriculture.

The story is told of the urban man who came to pastor the rural church. He was learning many new things as a newcomer to rural society. As he leaned on the fence and talked to Buster Hartley, he looked at the field and saw a cow. The pastor asked, "Buster, why is it that some cows have horns and some cows don't have horns?"

At the pastor's question, Buster looked at the pastor directly with a little bit of a quiver in his lower lip. "Well, Pastor," replied Buster, "there are several reasons that some cows have horns and others do not. One reason is that some cows naturally have horns and others don't. Some cows don't have horns because the farmer cuts them off. But the reason this cow doesn't have horns is because this cow is a horse!"

Unfortunately for John and Tris, as for this pastor, there was no class in rural ministry. They were not aware of any books or resources that might help them understand the rural setting. There was no rural orientation similar to the exposure their friend would get in missions school. They would have no opportunity to sort through their biases, assumptions, false expectations, and values concerning the ministry in which they had been placed. Unfortunately this would have an adverse effect on the effectiveness of their ministry. It would mean an extended time of adjustment. There would be tensions they would not understand. They would make assumptions, and assumptions would be made about them that would raise their frustration and the frustration level of the congregation.

If they had read any books on rural ministry, it is most likely that these resources would have subtly led them to believe that rural was a place. In fact, rural is a culture, a way of life. Once they understood that reality, it would provide them an open door to effective ministry.

John and Tris didn't realize it as they were driving toward North Dakota, but they were about to experience culture shock for the first time in their lives. They wouldn't understand it except in retrospect. What they were to experience would be fun, exciting, challenging, fearful, uncomfortable, painful, and exhilarating—all at the same time.

Beginning the Rural Pastorate

Pastor John and Tris arrived at the parsonage at Hudson just before dark. There was Don, the head deacon, ready to welcome them. Right away they noticed the personal touch that would characterize their ministry in this rural setting. He unlocked the parsonage, which was next to the church, and graciously showed them around. Don was an energetic, friendly, intelligent, high-tech farmer. Later, they would discover that he had a swimming pool and a satellite dish. They would also learn that he was heavily involved in real estate. Further, it would take them a few years to learn about the dominant and strong family of which Don was patriarch. It was a divisive element that had been a character flaw in this church for decades.

As they toured the parsonage kitchen, John and Tris were overwhelmed by the freezer filled with beef, cut by a local butcher and carrying the stamped names of several families that would become household words. The fruit cellar was stocked with canned peaches and pears, green beans and corn, and in the basement corner there was a large bushel basket full of potatoes.

When the moving van arrived the next day, 25 people were gathered at the parsonage through the quick telephone work of Caroline, Don's wife. John and Tris were both amazed at how quickly people could be gathered at 10:00 in the morning on a weekday. They were also amazed at how fast these folks worked and what good shape they were in.

The next day at 7:30 A.M., John leaped out of bed at the sound of the doorbell. Who could that be at this time in the morning? thought John to himself. What John didn't realize is that, in this setting, it could be just about anyone in their congregation. John slipped on his pants and went downstairs without socks or shirt. He opened the door, fully expecting to find a delivery man. Instead it was Dorothy Rue, whom he would come to love, respect, and appreciate as an elderly grandmother type within the congregation. "Hi, Pastor," Dorothy said with a smile that John would come to recognize as one of the most positive experiences visitors would have in his church. "My name is Dorothy Rue. It's not too early for you, is it?"

"No, not at all," said John as he "combed" his hair with the fingers of his hand.

Dorothy had come by to say hello and to set up the Communion for Sunday. She wanted Pastor John to come over and see if it was all right. John discovered she had been doing the Communion for 40 years, but she said the last pastor had made such a fuss over the way things should be laid out on the altar table that she was afraid to do it unless Pastor John checked it. Pastor John told her he was sure it was just fine and not to worry about it.

John invited Dorothy in and ran upstairs to find his shoes and a shirt. He was learning a lot about life in the congregation and about the way his predecessor majored in minors. Later he would discover that the previous pastor did not allow the people to do anything or give them any latitude to grow in their participation in ministry. John later became aware of one of the greatest temptations to the rural pastor: filling your calendar with the trivial and failing to focus on those things that most significantly contribute to the overall quality and quantity growth of the congregation.

John, as well as Tris, was in the middle of hundreds of experiences each day that would take him through the valley of the shadow of culture shock. It was a rural culture that they had never experienced. They had seen little vignettes of this culture, both accurate and inaccurate, in movies and on television. Over the next few months they would become experts.

One important principle for beginning a rural pastorate on a positive note is to recognize that you are joining history, and you must join history before you can make history. Many new pastors make the mistake of imposing their history upon the culture of the rural church. The independent nature of rural people and the tenacity they exhibit (which is both a strength and a weakness) will soon educate the pastor to the reality that he is the newcomer—even if he stays 10 years.

This is an important reality in the rural church, which has much more stability and less mobility than the church in an urban setting. Generally speaking, the rural church has a more stable constituency, and consequently, there is a shared history. The primary task for a new pastor is to learn that history, and the best way to do that is to listen.

It is generally true of seminary students. It is especially so for the student sent to the rural setting. The first 12 months in the parish should be considered the next 12 months of seminary training. In the rural setting, the primary objective is to learn the history of the congregation and to know what role individuals and families have in the dynamics of congregational life. If the new pastor is attentive, it should be fairly easy to discern who is the keeper of the oral tradition. In John's church, he soon discovered that it was Katherine, an elderly woman married to one of the elders of the church. She had a memory that John thought must be near the genius level. She could remember who did what and when and where for the last 60 years. And she was subconsciously training her daughter in the same tradition.

Some people thought Katherine a gossip. John saw her as a communicator. She would talk to just about anyone. Because of physical limitations, this was the way she socialized. For John, Katherine was a rich source of history and information concerning the church. He was careful, however, not to share anything negative or judgmental with her, lest he tempt her to be involved in gossip.

In the first few weeks of his ministry, he heard plenty of criticism of the previous pastor. He didn't know how much was true, nor did he care. But he soon found out from this that visiting the people in their homes was a high expectation of these people. Where he came from, people didn't expect visits from the pastor unless there was a serious problem. Usually, if someone wanted to see the pastor, he would make an appointment and meet at the church office. John quickly learned that the rural parsonage "office" had a drop-in-without-prior-notice policy. He and Tris made it a priority during the first few months to visit all the members in their homes.

This was one of the best things John could have done. He won the hearts of the people, and they responded positively to his personal care. He discovered that the people in this rural setting were likely to tell him many intimate family details on the first visit. This was very different from his experience in other settings. The details were so voluminous that he began making personal notes about each family so that he could remember what they had told him. In these notes he outlined the connections that people had with others in the congregation. He realized that many of the families were intricately related through in-law (and some "outlaw") structures. As he related to these people in the future, he communicated in ways that showed he remembered the details about their families. This made him one of the most popular pastors they had had for many decades.

In retrospect, John and Tris realized that their primary mission in the first year of their rural ministry was to study and adapt to the culture of the rural setting and to learn and join the history of the congregation.

The Relational Aspects of Rural Church Life

In many urban churches, the institutional or organizational dynamics of the church are very important. Committees have agendas, congregations have votes, boards have minutes. Church life and politics are fairly structured and usually task-oriented. Oftentimes, people on a board or committee will come together for monthly meetings and not have much relationship with the people gathered there beyond that meeting. What is more, they do not want a deeper relationship with those people.

In the rural setting, this is very different. A meeting scheduled to start at 8 P.M. may begin at 8:15 or even 8:30. Everyone may be there, but they may be talking about pork on the futures market or any number of other things. The personal relationships are a high priority. John soon learned this and began calling people by name as they came to each service. When he shook hands after worship, he was careful to call them by name. He realized that many decisions weren't made at the meetings but in the parking lot after church.

John began to change his traditional understanding of the Bible class. He realized this had to be a fellowship time as well as a learning time. He started by asking people what God had been doing in their lives. Then he asked for personal prayer requests. There might be as much as 20 minutes of relational activities at the beginning of the hour-long Sunday morning Bible class. The number of participants in the class grew to six times the size it was before John came.

With this understanding of the relational aspects in the church, John began small-group Bible studies. He let the people choose their own groups. Some met monthly at homes. Others met every two weeks at a restaurant in a nearby town.

He discovered that much of the business surrounding change took place over a meal. Because the rural community gets up early, there was a "breakfast culture" within the area. Consequently, he learned to get up earlier and to meet with many of the movers and shakers of the congregation, one-on-one, at breakfast settings.

The relational priority of people also made the annual church picnic more important than he had seen it in any other church. He made this a priority for ministry and looked forward to it every year. So did everyone in the church.

To build on this type of experience, John and Tris decided to have an annual barbecue at the parsonage. This turned out to be a much-anticipated outing for the members of the church and an excellent event to which they could invite prospective members.

The relational aspects of the church in the rural setting may be best symbolized by the fact that when the rural pastor visits a home of one of the members, he often enters (and is expected to) through the back door. In the task-oriented culture in which relationships are secondary, the pastor would most likely be expected to come more formally to the front door.

Fighting the "Temporary" Attitude

Many rural churches are accustomed to a parade of pastors, coming and going, each staying an average of about three years. Consequently, the church has a low self-image and is programmed to expect a high turnover of pastors.

The problem with short pastoral tenures is cyclical. Where pastors traditionally stay only a few short years, seminaries, publishing companies, and denominations offer few resources for the rural church pastor. With few resources, pastors are easily frustrated and are subtly told that this is not as important a ministry as somewhere else. So they move on quickly to another type of congregation, reinforcing the denomination's, seminary's, and publishing company's limited priority for the rural church. And the cycle goes on.

To break the cycle, seminaries need to identify the joys and challenges of ministry in a rural culture. If this was done in special classes, future pastors would begin to consider rural as an option instead of a white elephant door prize. Some seminary students would be encouraged to prepare specifically for a rural career.

If rural churches could experience the joy of long and positive pastoral tenures, it would build their self-esteem. The stronger self-esteem would help attract and hold the next pastor. This would reverse the cycle.

Just about the time John and Tris moved to Hudson, John inherited a piece of real estate in upstate New York. They put it on the market and eventually sold the property at a good price. John had been told many times at seminary that it was important for pastors who live in parsonages to invest in some kind of real estate. This was often the best way to build equity so that they could have a home when they retired and moved out of the parsonage. So John and Tris looked for property not too far away from Hudson. They expressed their commitment to stay in the area, but many of the members of the church were skeptical.

John and Tris took the money and made a down payment on a small ranch just a few miles south of the Hudson church. Many of the members of the church were amazed. No pastor in the long history of the church had ever made a commitment like that (with a 20-year mortgage!). In that way, John began to help change the worldviews of the congregation from a temporary mind-set. Of course, many other factors could move John to another ministry, but more than any previous pastor, John was making a statement of long-term commitment to the people.

Perspectives on Rural Leadership

A strong, focused, energetic pastoral leader is a part of the growth mix of any church. It is no different in the rural area. Leadership in the rural church is not only given with the title and role of "Pastor" but must be earned.

In a primarily white-collar congregation, the pastor often serves best as a team leader. In a blue-collar congregation, the pastoral style that works best could be described as a foreman leader. In some cases, an almost dictatorial leadership style can be used and is appreciated by the people. In other words, blue-collar people want strong leadership and do not mind being told what to do.

Frequently, the rural church calls for a relational leader. In the less mobile rural society, there are matriarchs and patriarchs who are active parts of extended families. Family members know well the importance of titles, order, rights, and privileges that go with status in life. So there is high respect for the pastoral office in many rural churches. If the church has had difficulty obtaining a pastor, or has lost pastors after a few years of ministry, there is a stronger incentive among people to follow the leader.

However, there is another leadership dynamic that is part of the mix for a rural church. Many involved in agricultural lifestyles are self-employed. They are used to making decisions without consulting anybody. Often, they are highly opinionated. Consequently, in the rural church a committee of one often works better than a committee of four or five. Within every extended farm family, there are dominant leaders and subordinate followers. It is important in the development of boards, committees, and ministry teams that dominant people from the same strong family do not serve on the same board. This would also be true of dominant people from different families.

John and Tris had only been serving the churches at Hudson and Agnes for a year and a half when John emerged with a leadership style that worked well for him. It could be described as a relational leadership style. There are many ways that John cultivated this style of leadership. When an important decision was to be made on a board or committee, John spent extra time meeting with each member of the board, in a relational setting. He cultivated and directed each person's thinking before the issue was raised in a group setting. One morning he had breakfast with Ron. That afternoon he saw Charlie mowing weeds across from his farmhouse and stopped and talked to him. The next day he had lunch with Michelle. Later that evening he stopped after dinner and talked with Jimmy and Linda. John didn't try to manipulate anyone. Nor was he playing politics. He was just cultivating the relationships that were part of the life-style of rural culture.

The biggest adjustment for John was to abandon his sense of agenda, which led him to want to start the meeting on time, stick to business, and leave the meeting as soon as work was finished. This task-oriented approach might work in a middle-sized church in Baltimore, but in the rural setting life was far different.

Building relationships takes time and effort. John worked hard at it. He was able to establish relationships that provided a context for progress in a congregation of independent farmers that held a high potential for division.

Once John earned his position of pastoral leader, most of the people followed. A unified ministry force for the benefit of the congregation was then established.

Leadership Toward Growth

Rural churches need pastors who are leaders with good attitudes: pastoral leaders who are in a rural setting because they want to be there and who are committed for a significant amount of time. These pastors/leaders will build a sound base for leadership that is intentionally relational.

There are at least six directives for pastoral leadership in the rural church that will help move the church toward quality and quantity growth.

1. *Vision casting.* The pastor will help mirror a vision to the members of the congregation. This is one of the primary objectives of any pastor in any congregation. It is particularly important in the rural setting in which factors like sparse population, long distances, lengthy membership tenure, or the business of the agricultural life can easily cloud the mission and ministry of a local church.

Pastors should help the people develop a clear, biblical understanding of who they are as God's people, what God has called the church to do and to be, and what opportunities for mission and ministry exist in the surrounding area. Basically, the pastor is constantly seeking to hone the worldviews of the people within the church to help them see with church growth eyes.

2. *Looking beyond.* The pastor who is leading the rural church toward growth will help the church look beyond itself. He will work with key leaders, opinion makers, and keepers of the oral tradition. He will influence families to move away from a self-centered perspective of the congregation to a balanced understanding of the church as a gathering form of community (which is healthy and profitable) and an equipping center to move out into the world. He will help them think about ways their church can be more effective in reaching unchurched in the community.

The pastor will help the congregation become visitor sensitive. This may include providing visitor parking, welcome signs, signs to the rest rooms, greeters at the door, a visitor friendly bulletin, etc. Of even deeper importance is a basic attitude of service and ministry to unchurched people who visit the church.

3. *Seeing the community.* The pastor can provide leadership to help the church diagnose itself and analyze its community. He will help the members identify the unchurched population in the

area. He will help members interview friends and neighbors to ascertain whether they are functionally churched or unchurched.

As the pastor leads the church toward seeing the community, he will help them identify their place in the immediate region. Is the church in the best location? Should it move? Are signs needed at major roads to direct people to the church? Does the church use area newspapers to help people identify its presence in the area?

4. *Setting goals for growth.* The pastor who is providing leadership in the rural church will help the congregation measure its effectiveness and develop a sense of accountability. How effective is the Vacation Bible School? How can we measure that effectiveness? What has been our growth in adult Sunday School over the last five years? What goals can we set for next year? The next five years? The next 10 years?

The pastor will lead each area of the church to develop its own goals. The Sunday School department can have goals. The youth can have goals. There can be stewardship goals and evangelism goals. Worship goals and membership goals are possible.

5. *Cheerleading.* The pastor who leads the rural church toward growth will cheer for the congregation as a regular part of pastoral duties. Laypeople in rural churches respond positively to encouragement, edifying, and building up. One of the key roles of a pastor as leader is to build the corporate self-esteem of the congregation.

The pastor will encourage people when they feel discouraged. He will thank those who have provided ministry and help in some way. He will challenge and coax people to try what others have said might be impossible. He will stretch their understanding of their own capabilities, individually and as a congregation.

6. *In for the long haul.* The pastor's long-term commitment will help the church develop long-term goals and plans. The pastor will form a leadership team of laypeople that look toward the future—not just the coming months, but the coming decade.

The pastor will continually communicate a commitment to a career and vocation in that setting. The pastor will let people know that he or she is there by choice, not because he or she was run-ner-up in a race with another pastor for a suburban congregation.

The pastor will put down roots in the community and pro-vide whatever visible symbols possible to signify the long-term commitment to this body of Christ in the rural setting.

Leadership in the Growing Ghost Town

To talk about a growing ghost town is a contradiction in terms. A ghost town is a town that is running out of people. This was discussed earlier under the subject of the shrinking church. It is included here because leadership in this particular kind of rural setting is unique.

The pastoral leadership of the shrinking church can lead to-ward growth. It may not be growth in numbers, but it may in-clude growth in personal discipleship, fellowship, and multipli-cation of churches.

There are many areas that experience a significant out-mi-gration of people due to loss of jobs, changing agricultural pat-terns, and other factors beyond the control of any pastor or con-gregation. It is common for the second generation to move to different areas for educational purposes or employment. Mean-while, the first and older generation becomes fewer because the death rate continues, and there is no influx of new people. Lead-ership in this setting has its own challenges.

The first challenge to the pastor in this setting is to conduct a serious, in-depth, long-range study of demographic trends. Sometimes it seems that the population is declining, when actu-ally it is just changing. In the Seymore Church in the northwest United States, it appeared as though there was no future for the area. Most of the people of the church were connected with the lumber industry, and the source of available timber had been de-pleted. Many timber workers were moving elsewhere.

However, the Seymore area was experiencing a growth in recreational activities. The church had not responded to the new people coming into the area. While the trend was not significant, an in-depth study with the Chamber of Commerce, county and state governments, census tracts, and industry analysts, reflected that while short-term growth of the population was limited, the in-migration of people to the area in the next 10 years would be quite outstanding. The church did not need to concentrate on dying. It needed to be led to survive in the short term, and to change over the next several years in preparation for future growth.

But what about the church that is in the declining population area that shows no reversal or change in the future? In this setting the pastoral leader is charged with the important ministry of helping the church die with dignity. This type of ministry includes several factors.

1. *Remove guilt.* The pastor/leader is called in the caretaking ministry to help people recognize that the demise of the church is beyond their control—if that is indeed the reality. When the population of an area is declining, has declined over a period of time, and is expected to continue to decline, the people must realize that no pastor or congregation can change the social forces in motion at that time in history. People should not feel there is something wrong with them.

2. *Commit to ministry as long as possible.* Usually this becomes a financial issue. Study the realities. Help the people understand the limitations and commit to ministering to them for as long as it is feasible.

3. *Face reality.* Help the people recognize that if present trends continue there will come a time when the church will close. As you graph the decline based on the last 5 to 10 years, you may be able to project when the church might close. During this time, challenge the people to give sacrificially to sustain ministry as long as possible, but balance that with sensitive stewardship that recognizes when a good use of resources becomes an abuse of resources. There comes a time when enough is enough. The pastoral leader can help the people recognize and accept that reality.

4. *Build a healthy sense of pride.* Help the people be proud of their ministry, their heritage, and their history. Help them celebrate with thanksgiving each day the Lord gives them to minister. Encourage them to resist the temptation to seek denominational subsidy to prolong the inevitable demise of the congregation.

Help them realize that such subsidy monies could be deployed elsewhere in ministry to reach people for Jesus Christ.

5. *Consider long-range alternatives.* Help the members of the church consider what will happen after the church closes. Can a house-church ministry be provided? Can the people combine with members of another church and bring health and support to that church or perhaps help prolong its ministry in the same declining population area? Meet with other churches and discuss what could be done by coming together or using shared facilities or shared pastoral leadership.

6. *Have a homecoming party.* Set a date before the church becomes too small and too weak, and invite all the previous members of the church to come share in one last celebration of ministry. Invite a special speaker who will reflect positively on the wonderful history God has provided in the ministry of the congregation. Ask people to bring photographs representing the history of the congregation. Provide displays of the congregation's accomplishments through its years of ministry.

7. *Hold a going out of business sale.* Pastoral leadership is helpful in this delicate and challenging aspect of church death. People need to be led to understand that the resources that have provided furniture, equipment, and real estate belong to God, not the individuals who gave them. How can these things be sold to provide the most resources for ministry in God's kingdom elsewhere?

8. *Help the church prepare a spiritual will.* This would be a document that would promise the assets, once liquidated, to provide a mission and ministry start in some other area, either nearby or overseas.

Whether in the rural church with a potential for growth or in the declining population area, leadership is a key. It is a unique style of leadership, in many ways, with many challenges and opportunities far different from what another setting might provide. One of the areas that is of critical importance for pastoral leadership, and lay leadership alike, is the area of worship in the rural church.

7

Worship in the Rural Church

Maxine had once had loose connections with the Milford
Chapel, but her husband had not been interested in church. He
had died several years ago, but her habit of missing church did
not change, though she thought about it many times.

One morning, Pastor Fritz was interrupted from his sermon
preparation by a phone call from Sandra. Sandra was a neighbor
of Maxine's and had known her for a long time. Since Pastor Fritz
had come to the church, he had helped her obtain church growth
eyes. She had called about Maxine. When she asked if the pastor
knew her, he responded that he had not even heard of her.

"I've been trying to encourage Maxine to get to church late-
ly," said Sandra. "I just heard that her son was killed in an air-
plane accident. I think she needs a pastor. I called and asked if
she would mind if I called you. She sounded like she would be
really happy if you would visit her."

That was the beginning of ministry to Maxine at a very trag-
ic and difficult time in her life. Over the months that followed,
she blossomed into a growing, excited, active Christian.

Worship became one of the most central parts of her life. She
considered the church members to be her family. She would never
forget their kindness, love, and support during her difficult time.

For Maxine, worship was a time to give praise to God. It was
a time to learn about God. But more than that, it was a time to relate with other people who had become an integral part of her life.

Sunday worship, as the term is used here, is that total Sunday morning experience. It is everything that happens in the time

that a person like Maxine enters the church property until she says good-bye to her friends with whom she has Sunday dinner.

In the rural setting, worship is often more central and more important than it is in many other churches. Because relationships are so important, the task of ministry, often symbolized by activities and programs in other churches, is signified by the relational aspect of life in the rural church. The weekly worship gathering is particularly significant to the rural community.

Second, the population is often (not always) scattered over a larger distance than the church in a suburban or urban setting. Consequently, members may not see each other as much during the week. In churches in other settings, the members may see each other at the office or factory or touch each others' lives at PTA, the YMCA, or Little League.

A third factor that helps make worship more central in the rural-oriented church is the lower mobility of many rural areas. Since people don't move around as much, there is a higher frequency of intergenerational demographics within the rural church. When people in the agriculture come to church, they often see their parents, grandparents, children, and grandchildren, as well as their aunts and uncles, cousins, and other shirttail relatives. Consequently, worship in the rural church can be a weekly, extended-family, family reunion.

A fourth reason that some rural churches find worship more central is that they are smaller. The smaller church would have less ministry programs and activities. Therefore worship is, relatively, a higher priority.

In churches with shared pastors, the smaller church may see the minister only for worship. The worship setting, then, becomes the only time the worship community is gathered together. In the absence of other activities, the worship setting is much more central and important.

Worship and Communication

Rural culture is an open culture. It is common for people who pass one another on the road to wave and say hello to everyone they meet. In an urban setting, such behavior would be totally unacceptable. For a man to say "hi" to a woman would raise certain suspicions. To say it to a man, in the age in which we now live, would also raise suspicions. People in cities pass on the sidewalk without saying a word to each other. In a rural setting, that would not be the case.

In many settings, the work and the tasks set the agenda. In a rural setting, it is much more likely that people set the agenda. For example, Jeff was busy repairing his manure spreader. Brad Creel stopped by to borrow a generator. Jeff wanted to work on his manure spreader because it was time to clean the barnyard. But when Brad stopped, the work stopped. Brad talked about the weather, the need for a local veterinarian that could specialize in cattle breeding, and the recent performance of the Chicago Cubs. Jeff let Brad set the agenda, not the task of his manure spreader.

Another example of the open culture of the rural setting is the drop-in visit. Appointments, or agreements to meet, are not necessary. If the person is not home, it's not considered a wasted trip as it would be in other cultural settings. If the person is home, the drop-in visit is totally acceptable. Of course, the people who are being visited are busy. Everyone is busy. But the visit preempts the work. The work is never done anyway. If it is delayed, what's the difference? (The only exception to this is during planting time and harvesttime, when the weather sets the agenda.) Sunday afternoons are often set aside for two major purposes: eating and visiting.

These communication realities in the rural culture have numerous implications for worship, which is a strong communication ministry. Invitations to church are much *easier* than in many other types of churches. People can be more responsive to invitations to "Friend Day" or "Bring a Friend Sunday." This means that strategies in which the church invites neighbors to come to share in its ministries, from worship to ice cream socials, are much more important for the rural church.

Another implication is that a good first impression is important. People are expecting a friendly church made up of their friendly neighbors from the friendly rural setting. In urban or suburban churches, particularly larger churches, friendliness is not as strongly expected by the visitor. After all, many of those people live in a world where they ride in the proximity of an elevator and never speak to other people. Why should strangers at church talk to them in a setting like that?

A third implication for communication in worship is that communication *among* the people in the worship setting is as important as communication *from* the pastor. Opportunities for communication among people in worship are very important. If people talk with each other before worship begins, it is not a disrespect for the house of God. This is a family reunion. Who would ever go to a family reunion and sit piously without talking to anyone?

A fourth implication for worship and communication is that the Bible class is part of the Sunday morning worship experience. It is an important form for meeting communication needs. Bible class should provide many opportunities for dialogue and interaction among the people.

Communication in the rural setting is more verbal than written. This has great implications for many aspects of the church, including the fact that rural church people are generally less responsive to receiving a letter than a visit or a phone call.

People in a rural setting rely on the telephone for much of their verbal communication. Most urbanites would be absolutely amazed if they knew how much the telephone is used among rural neighbors.

Verbal communication has implications for worship too. For one thing, name tags (written communication) are probably less appropriate. The Sunday bulletin may have less verbiage in the rural church. Announcements ought to be more verbal than written. Furthermore, announcements can be less church-to-people-oriented and more people-to-people-oriented. In the less formal setting of the rural church, it would be appropriate for the pastor to ask if anyone has announcements to share with the group.

Relational Implications for Worship

Since the rural culture has a strong emphasis on relationships, the seating arrangement may appropriately be a semicircle or fan shape, instead of the typical northern European classroom style. If the worship setting means community, what better way to demonstrate it than to sit in a way that allows people to see each other face-to-face?

Many liturgical churches practice what is called the "handshake of peace." This is a remnant of the New Testament kiss of peace. People should be given opportunity to wander all over the church. A rural pastor could allow as much as 5 to 10 minutes for people to say hello and share God's love with others in the sanctuary.

Another characteristic of liturgical churches is the presence of an altar. It would be more necessary to have a free-standing altar in which the worship leader can face the people in a rural church.

In many church settings the pastor says "Good morning," and the congregation responds. This brief opportunity for dialogue is most appropriate in the rural church.

From the relational standpoint, it is good for the choir and musicians to be in the front of the church when providing music so that there is face-to-face contact. The pulpit, lectern, or podium that is used by the preacher is less important in the open culture of the rural church. It is more important for the preacher to be face-to-face.

Preaching in the rural church is aided by the imagery of Scripture, which is often agriculturally oriented. The Bible offers many images that fit the rural scene: the Vine and the branches, the sheep, the sower, the harvest, the vineyard, and many more.

In the New Testament, many images reflect the Church. These include the kingdom of God, the citizens of the Kingdom, the priesthood of all believers, the children of God, and many more. Perhaps the best of these images for the relational, community-oriented worship of the rural church is the family of God.

Special Celebrations

Pastor Elsham had been at the Heather Community Bible Church only two weeks when a young couple stopped by to set a date for their wedding.

The church that he had previously pastored in Louisville

was primarily made up of members who were involved in the excavation business. When someone got married there, a few friends and family members attended the wedding ceremony. In the rural setting of Heather Community, he was shocked when he discovered the church overflowing, not only with friends and relatives but with just about every member of the church. It looked like Sunday and then some.

Often, weddings and funerals in the rural setting are extensions of Sunday morning worship, plus a community get-together. The implications for worship preparation are obvious. Additionally, this is a great opportunity for the pastor—particularly a new pastor—to woo potential members to the church. It is a great time to preach the gospel and the basics of salvation to some in the community who desperately need to hear it.

The church would develop its best prospect list by obtaining the names of those people in attendance, identifying those who live within the ministry area of the church who are unchurched. These prospects could receive an invitation to special worship activities, ice cream socials, Christmas or Easter services, musical programs, and to Vacation Bible School.

Since weddings and funerals in the rural church are special celebrations, it is good to encourage the receptions following these events to be held at the church if the facilities allow. In fact, it is ideal for the rural church to have a good fellowship hall (multipurpose room) for this ministry. It is important to involve laypeople in the congregation when providing food and services for the ceremony. It is important for the pastor to take advantage of the opportunity for mixing with the crowd. It is good if the church can provide the use of its facilities at no cost for weddings and funerals.

Another ministry that capitalizes on the unique characteristics of the rural church is the encouragement for married couples to renew their marriage vows in an anniversary celebration at the church. Friends and neighbors are invited. This program underscores the importance of solid marriages and opens the door to many visitors. It also provides a forum for relational activity centered around the life of the church.

Family reunions provide another opportunity for the church in the rural setting to minister to extended families. When the Schmidt family had their yearly family reunion at the Waterbury Church, Pastor Perryman had his annual opportunity to see inactive members, Harold and Dolores Schmidt. The cultivation of this relationship paid off one year later when Harold and Dolores were involved in a serious auto accident. Ultimately, they became active in the worship life of the congregation. Family reunions may also provide an opportunity to offer a brief worship service as part of the activities. This gives the pastor an opportunity to preach the good news about Jesus Christ and may lead to contact with unchurched relatives who live within the ministry area of the congregation.

Civic events and community affairs are occasions for the church to serve its rural neighbors. The Wentzville Church worked hard to be the polling place for their precinct. The church offered coffee and pie to the people after they voted.

The church at Grange provided facilities for the Alcoholics Anonymous group for Branch County. Each time they met, church members would provide a snack and update the church bulletin board that was located in the room.

The House of Prayer Community in Hamilton provided a semiannual blood bank in cooperation with the Red Cross. On alternate months they provided free blood pressure checks for anyone in the area.

There are many activities the church can provide for the rural community. If the congregation is trained with "church growth eyes," it will capitalize on opportunities to meet the needs of people. At the same time, it will provide avenues through which they can hear the good news of Jesus Christ and respond to an invitation to become a part of the Body of Christ.

Worship for Growth

Jack and Judy were the parents of three lovely children. As the children grew, they were continual reminders of the spiritual responsibilities that Jack and Judy had toward them and toward themselves. Since Jack's open-heart surgery, the realities of life and death had become more prominent in their minds. They felt that they should start attending church regularly.

Jack remembered that a friend had mentioned a church just north of Turkey Lake. They decided to try it the next Sunday. As they drove to the church the next week, they felt a little uncomfortable, as most people do who visit a church as strangers. Jack had miscalculated the distance, so they were late. The parking lot was full, so he dropped the family at the front door and parked at the far end of the lot. By the time he caught up with his family, his shoes were muddy.

Judy thought the usher gave them a strange look and felt even more uncomfortable. They were handed bulletins without comment. The service was already started, and there were no seats in the back rows. They had to go way up front.

The worship service was hard for them to follow. It seemed as if everyone else knew when to stand and when to sit, but because they were in the front, it was difficult to follow the rest of the crowd. After the sermon, the pastor announced that Communion would be served. People started going forward. Judy couldn't decide whether it would be offensive to go like the others or whether it would be offensive not to go.

After church the pastor shook their hands and said hello, but he didn't ask if they were visitors, where they were from, or what their names were. Jack and Judy left feeling like they had intruded on someone's private family affair.

It was six months before the Spirit moved Jack and Judy to try church again. This time they went to Zion near Waterloo. They arrived before the service began. They had phoned earlier and learned the location of the church. Neither of them were familiar with that area, but they were told there would be a large sign for the church on the corner of a certain street.

There seemed to be a lot of cars for a country church surrounded by corn and soybean fields. As they entered the parking lot, there was a young man directing traffic. The man directed them to some spots near the front door marked "Visitors Parking." As they got out of the car, a young lady welcomed them with a big smile.

When they entered the church, they received a warm welcome from the greeters. Then Rebecca welcomed them and introduced herself. When she discovered this was their first visit, she offered to sit with them and help them through the service.

After worship, Rebecca invited them to the adult Bible class. They were hesitant, but Rebecca said she would sit with them and also took the family to the office to find a class for each of the children. The children were taken to class and introduced to several of the other children. Before the children knew it, they were involved as part of the group.

At the adult Bible class, everyone was enjoying juice, coffee, and cookies. Rebecca introduced them to several other members of the class. Soon the pastor came in from the sanctuary, and the crowd quieted down and took seats. The room was set up with tables and chairs so that everyone could see everyone else.

After greeting Jack and Judy and a few other visitors, the pastor asked the class to share what God was doing in their lives. As some interesting testimonies were given, Jack thought, God sure is real in everyday life to these people. After a few other opening remarks, the pastor asked for prayer requests, which were listed on the overhead projector. Jack noticed that several of the members wrote these prayer requests in a notebook.

The pastor taught from the Bible, and there was a lot of discussion in the class, which he encouraged. After the class was dismissed, Rebecca took Jack and Judy to find their children. She invited Jack and Judy and their family to lunch at the Brass Lantern with the Seiberts and herself and pointed out that there were some free lunch coupons in the visitor's packet they had received. During lunch they had an opportunity to talk about the worship experience and the friendliness of the church.

That evening as Jack and Judy were finishing supper, the doorbell rang. It was Karen Heigartner and her husband, Dean. They remembered Karen because she had played the piano in the adult Sunday School class. Karen and Dean were out making calls on the people who had visited the church that day and simply wanted to tell them how glad they were that they came to church and hoped they would come back again.

As Karen and Dean turned to walk toward their car, Jack said without any hesitation, "Thanks for stopping by. See you next Sunday."

Were there any differences between the church at Turkey Lake and the one near Waterloo? There are many areas in which there are no differences between the Turkey Lake church and the church near Waterloo. God is God in both churches. God wants to use both churches to touch the lives of people like Jack and Judy. The Holy Spirit is present in both churches. God is the one who builds His kingdom, by the power of His Spirit working in people's lives. That is the same in both churches.

Both churches have true believers. Both churches have people who are saved and who know the Lord and who are going to be with Him eternally. Both churches believe and teach the Bible. Both follow high Christian moral and ethical standards. Both churches have some inactive members. Both churches have problems. Both churches have negative members. Both pastors have their strengths and weaknesses. Both congregations would say that they believe in the Great Commission to make disciples of all peoples. Yes, in many ways, both of these churches are the same. However, in many obvious ways these churches are different, particularly from the perspective of Jack and Judy and their children.

Which church is growing? That's not a difficult guess. Zion Church near Waterloo is a rural church that understands the principles of worship for growth. These principles are part of the general attitude that people have toward the mission of their church and their outreach to the unchurched. Three key areas for growth are important.

1. *Developing an attraction model.* The rural church that capitalizes on its worship opportunities attracts visitors and holds them, just like a magnet.

Zion Church does this through focusing on the community aspects of the worship setting. Jack and Judy experienced community the moment they drove into the parking lot. That community continued not only in worship but also in Sunday School, at lunch, and later that evening when Dean and Karen visited their home. Everything about the church reflected community.

Another way of developing an attraction model is to advertise and publicize. For the rural church, this is often much easier and less expensive than for a church in a metropolitan area. Most local newspapers in small towns or county newspapers will readily accept well-prepared news articles from local churches.

One year the pastor of Zion Church remembered that many people said they felt like Christmas came and went much too fast. He developed a plan to celebrate Christmas in July. All the local newspapers from the area publicized the service. A large crowd appeared for the worship service in which the pastor preached on the Christmas theme, the children provided some skits of the story of the birth of Jesus, the Christmas tree glistened with tinsel and lights, and the congregation sang "Joy to the World." Zion Church worked creatively and hard to publicize the ministry and encourage others to know about their work.

A congregation also can develop an attraction model by training the people to bring their friends. Recent research conducted by the Church Growth Center shows that in many churches most new members will *tell* 25 or more people about their new church home. They will *invite* between 8 and 12 people to attend their new church home. However, the majority of new members will *bring* between 0 and 4 people to their new church home. The key is to train members to identify receptive friends and neighbors, to know when they are receptive, to know what to do and say to lead toward a witness, and to lead toward an invitation to join them in attendance at their church. An excellent program to train members to do this is *Heart to Heart: Sharing Christ with a Friend*.

2. *Becoming visitor sensitive.* Being sensitive to visitors is an important part of worship in the growing rural church. Visitor sensitivity begins with signs that help locate the church. Many rural churches are located in out-of-the-way places and hard-to-find locations. Consequently, the rural church often has a special challenge to provide signs in all four directions from the church. Visitor sensitivity continues with providing ample parking, clean

parking lots, visitor parking, traffic directors, and parking lot greeters.

Visitor sensitivity includes signs within the building that point to the bathrooms, the fellowship hall, the sanctuary, the Sunday School office, and any other important point in the building.

Being sensitive to visitors, congregational members will provide spaces near the back and near the aisle. Subconsciously, visitors want to know that if something uncomfortable happens, they can get out quickly. Having a few members who will make it their ministry on Sunday morning to sit with visitors and help them through the worship service is also an important part of visitor sensitivity.

Providing a readable bulletin is another way to show consideration to visitors. Many church bulletins have all sorts of abbreviations and in-house language that make it impossible for the visitor to understand what is being said. This implies that the church does not really care whether visitors know what they're doing in church.

Another area of importance to the visitor is the friendliness of the congregation. It's amazing, but a church can appear friendly through the efforts of only 6 to 10 people who make it their commitment to meet and greet people. Many churches have greeters. Additionally, churches ought to have greeter commandos. These are people who, incognito—without the badge and the bulletins—will make a ministry effort on Sunday morning to look for, identify, and encourage visitors.

3. *Need for follow-up.* The third important area of worship for growth is the follow-up mechanism that a church maintains. It is important to get the name, address, and telephone number of first-time visitors in a nonembarrassing, nonthreatening way. It is also helpful to know if they have a church home and whether they are active in their church. The best way to find out if they are active is to ask them the name of their pastor. If they don't know the name of their pastor but record a church home, chances are they are not very active.

Many churches obtain this information through the use of a

friendship pad. This is a pad that is passed down the row for everyone to fill out. This helps keep visitors from feeling like they are on the spot.

Immediate follow-up is important. This is an aspect of assimilation that is often overlooked by churches. You will remember that the Seiberts and Rebecca took Jack and Judy and their children to lunch. This is an extremely important time after the visitors come to their first worship service. There is always a debriefing time in people's minds after they experience something. If you can help them work through that debriefing time, answer questions, and encourage the assimilation further, it will hasten the familiarity process. Zion Church near Waterloo uses free dinner coupons from the Brass Lantern Restaurant. Maranatha Christian Fellowship in Greensboro is housed in a refurbished elementary school and uses the lunchroom as a church-run restaurant called the Agape Restaurant. The food is good, and it is inexpensive (because it is offered as a nonprofit ministry). Visitors at Maranatha receive a packet with free coupons to the Agape Restaurant. This gives them the opportunity to have fellowship and meet a few more people who are members of the church.

Another means of follow-up is a visit to the home. This is particularly helpful if done within 24 hours and if initiated by members of the church, rather than the pastor.

Often, pastors will follow up with a phone call during the week. This can be helpful and might be the best, nonthreatening way for the pastor to make an initial contact.

Another way of follow-up is by letter. Many churches send a letter to visitors within a week of the visit.

A pastoral visit is particularly advantageous in a rural area in which relational aspects of the culture are strong. If members are making a visit at the home the first week, it is probably best for the pastor to make his visit to the people attending a second time.

Another key strategy in follow-up is to invite new prospects to a home Bible study. This is perhaps the most powerful strategy of follow-up and assimilation that a church can use.

Finally, if the church has a new members' class, a pastor's

class for new membership, or some other mechanism for joining the church, it is important that some system of follow-through be made and monitored so that people would be invited to join at the appropriate time.

The whole worship experience is more important than perhaps any other aspect of church life. The pastor and the laypeople in the rural church can justify an extraordinary amount of time and energy in making the worship experience the best it can be.

8

Rural Church Finances

*I*t was late June in 1886 when Pastor Jon Bender first came to the Fair Oaks Congregational Church. Jon and his wife, Evelyn, came by train from the East where Jon had received his seminary training.

When Jon and Evelyn reached the parsonage, they were greeted by Elder David Longweil. The arrangement that had been developed through letters was now consummated by a handshake. Pastor Bender and Evelyn had the full use of the parsonage, a horse, a buggy, and a small barn. The church would provide seven ranks of seasoned wood annually; a cow; seeds for a vegetable garden; oats, hay, and straw for the horse; and meat and poultry when it was needed and when it was butchered. In addition to this, Jon received a few dollars, which was paid monthly.

Financial Changes

Rural life has changed dramatically in the last 100 years. One of the most dramatic changes is that it has moved from an economy that was based on payment in kind and/or remuneration by service to a money economy. But this change is mixed, and it has been slow.

Today's farmer is much more likely to pay money to a regional company to put up a pole building than he is to gather the neighbors together to put up the barn. Neighbors do help one another, particularly at the busy times of the year—planting and harvesting. But the remuneration for that work is usually based on a cash exchange. Often, one farmer will specialize in certain equipment to do a certain task. Besides farming his own farm, he will provide custom work for other farmers. This, too, is usually done on a hire basis.

There are some remnants of the old economy. The rural church is likely to pay the pastor less in cash. The pastor may be asked to live in a parsonage with a garden in the backyard.

Church cleaning is sometimes a paid job, but more likely it will be accomplished by volunteers. Maintenance is usually done by a group of trustees or a building and grounds committee. The parking lot is plowed in the winter by one of the men. The organist and the choir director are most likely volunteers or are paid very minimally. These are all remnants of a former rural economy.

Rural Cash Flow

The great uncertainty of income as well as the enormous fluctuations in amounts of income from year to year make it difficult for a congregation to budget. Pledging dollar amounts is almost an impossibility for the rural church.

If the rural church is involved in a pledge system at all, it should be by percentage giving, which is the biblical way, anyway. It is far better and particularly suited to people who do not know their income from year to year.

Unique Challenges

There are at least eight challenges in the area of finances that greatly affect the life and ministry of the rural church.

1. *Attitude.* The attitude of many agriculturally oriented people is that they are poor. That is what they say. However, that is not what they mean. In reality, most agricultural people are not poor. They are cash poor. In other words, their assets are not liquid.

Many rural people have difficulty paying their bills because they owe the bank several thousand dollars for a combine. Or they may be in debt to the Land Bank for another 80 acres they just added to their growing homestead, or they owe several hundred dollars to their brothers and sisters so that they can finally own the family farm. They are often wealthy people. But their money is tied up in land, buildings, equipment, seed, fertilizer,

cattle, timber, and many other aspects of the extremely complicated financial picture of agricultural life today.

The obvious challenge to the rural church is that, while
there is no problem getting the parking lot plowed when it
snows or the building cleaned on a weekly basis, it's difficult to
pay the electric bill or the minister's pension fund. The lack of
liquid assets on the farm is also a reality at the church.

2. *Financial planning is impossible.* It is extremely difficult for
the church to make long-range financial plans. The people are
unsure of their income. In the complexities of rural life, income
can be greatly affected by the rising cost of herbicide, rain at the
right time in Kansas, the price of oil, next year's Farm Bill, late
CRP (Conservation Reserve Program) payments, or an article in
the *New England Journal of Medicine* about some new health problem caused by eating beef.

The volatile nature of the agricultural world makes it almost
ludicrous for well-meaning Christians to make long-range pre-
dictions concerning their income and their ability to invest specific amounts in God's kingdom. The rural church, therefore, has
an extremely difficult challenge to plan ahead and to be a good
manager of the financial resources the Lord may or may not provide.

3. *Sporadic income.* Income in the rural culture is received
occasionally. It can be the result of the sale of cattle, harvest of
grain, fruit or vegetable harvest, sale of timber, or, increasingly,
the sale of a portion of property. Many agricultural people are in
the real estate business, but they don't know it. This is particularly true of rural areas that are identified with strong growth potential. In any given year, some farmers will make more money
on the sale of a portion of their property, or the entire sale of
their property, than they have made cumulatively over the last 25
years.

Whenever comparing per capita giving trends within a congregation, the church must do so over long periods of time due
to the enormous fluctuations of occasional income. Further, the
data of per capita giving must be refined significantly. Questions
must be asked to ascertain why per capita giving peaked at one

time or was low at another. What else was happening across the landscape of the agriculture?

Biblical stewardship is an extremely important part of the economic health of the church in the rural area. It is important for the people to understand the principle of percentage giving. For example, Bob had a farm all of his life. He also tithed—he gave 10 percent of his income to the work of the Lord through his church. Some years his giving was low; other years it was somewhat higher, depending upon his income. During the drought several years ago, his giving was minimal—almost nothing at all. He was strictly practicing the percentage method of giving: giving as the Lord had given to him. When Bob sold a portion of his farm last year for $300,000, he practiced consistent Christian stewardship. The church received $30,000 for the work of the Lord.

Another implication for the rural church is the importance of setting up a foundation for large sums of money such as the gift given by Bob. This foundation should not be a mechanism by which the church saves and invests money only to spend the interest. God has not called the church to be a bank. The foundation should be a means through which the church manages and administrates the timing of the expenditures and receipts of monies for the best stewardship of resources.

4. *Financially conservative.* As independent businesspeople in high-risk activity, with a multitude of variables affecting their income, rural people have to be financially conservative or they won't survive.

In the 1800s, the rural financial conservatism was shown by money stored in the cookie jar or wrapped in an old sock under the mattress or hidden in a fruit jar in the cellar. Today money is tied up in certificates of deposit (CDs). This is money that rural people put away "just in case." This is not a weakness; it is a way of survival.

Financial conservatism has several implications for the rural church. First, it is very important for the church to plan well for any new church project. This is particularly true for projects such as the purchase of an organ, the building of a fellowship hall, or the development of a day-care center. It is important to know all the costs, including the "hidden" costs.

Second, it is important to finish the project under budget. When a project is costed, the established figure should include latitude for unforeseen expenses. It is much better to finish the project on target or under budget than it is to spend more than was at first communicated.

Third, process the decision. Take a *long* time to cultivate the project. Plan the project, not by the month, but in a seasonal time frame.

Fourth, if there is fund-raising involved, make sure the timing is the proper point in the calendar year that matches the agricultural income in your area. The money comes in after the harvest. The church should plan accordingly.

Fifth, remember that large donations (usually anything over $500) do not come out of the spendable, discretionary income of individuals. Most individuals tap their accumulated wealth (the CDs) for this type of giving.

Sixth, communicate the project thoroughly. Utilize relational communication forums. Capitalize on the power of communication through the keeper of the oral tradition.

Seventh, communicate conceptually. If the project is to capture the imagination of the people, the best way to demonstrate its value is through pictures, not just words. At Beulah Church in Clear Creek, the pastor and a few lay leaders developed a videotape presentation to communicate the need for a new fellowship hall. On the videotape they showed the need by taking footage of the overcrowded conditions in the adult Sunday School class. They also showed where the building would be built. They included shots of a drawing of the building. They interviewed key leaders in the congregation who were highly respected and who were supportive of the project. Then they took this videotape to all the homes of the people, asking them to participate.

5. *Income in kind.* Another challenge unique to the rural church is that many of the people receive blessings from God that never get translated into cash. The people in agricultural areas often heat with their own wood and eat fruit from their own

trees, vegetables from their own garden, and meat from their own cattle. The positive implication is that an inflationary economy may not affect giving to the church as much as it would among people who directly purchase goods and services.

How does the Christian return a portion of these blessings to the Lord's work? This is an area where the rural church can sensitize people to think in stewardship terms beyond a financial economy. Since the Lord asks us to bless Him in proportion to the way He has blessed us, how do we return a portion of that blessing when, for example, we have saved $450 in heating bills because God has blessed us with an abundance of wood in the northwest corner of the farm? Can the rural church sensitize the Christian to understand that the realized saving is a blessing from God that could be reflected in a $45.00 boost to our offerings? How does the church direct and motivate the Christian to joyfully respond with such a gift when that person is already *cash* poor? How can such an understanding of thanksgiving be tied to occasional large gifts from accumulated wealth sources that are associated with special projects?

6. *What is a profit?* In the agricultural business, like any self-employed business, reinvestment is important for future health and vitality of the business. It is also tax deductible. Consequently, agricultural people often show a loss (for tax purposes) or, at best, very little profit. This is both legal and proper. Yet, paradoxically, at the same time the net worth of the individual grows. How does the Christian handle this issue of what is real income for the purposes of stewardship and the giving of offerings? Should the percentage that is chosen to pledge to God be based on gross income or net income?

7. *Market profits.* Many agriculturally oriented people do not have the benefit of a retirement program. Consequently, those who are most disciplined regularly put money away in stocks and bonds. Sometimes this is in an individual retirement account (IRA) or some other savings program. In addition to this, many people involved in agriculture will take some of the profits of a good year and invest it in the stock market or the futures market.

This provides a challenge to any church, but it may be a greater challenge to the rural church because of the number of people who would be involved in such a savings program. The challenge is to help individuals recognize that when they take a profit on investments, that profit is a blessing from God and a percentage gift to the work of the Lord is appropriate. It is helpful for the church to encourage members to respond as good stewards at times when investments reach maturity or when they make out their wills.

8. *Accumulated wealth and the Christian will.* Since many Christians in agriculture are cash poor and real estate rich, it is important to help them recognize the importance of providing a Christian will. A Christian's will not only gives testimony to faith in Jesus Christ but also provides for the Lord's work through a Christian displacement of assets. There are numerous stories in Christian ministry today reflecting the enormous impact that a major gift has had on a specific ministry.

If the family farm (or a part of it) is sold at the time of death, what provision is there for the work of the Lord? Does the Lord's work receive a percentage of the assets in thanksgiving to God?

Throughout history, Christian mission and ministry has often been hampered by lack of finances. This is yet another area in which the rural church has an opportunity to help Christians show their faith, even after death.

The Annual Bazaar

To deal with the subject of a bazaar in the rural church is to live dangerously. Many denominations do not allow bazaars. The subject is especially sensitive in rural churches. For our purposes, let us consider bazaars as only a *symbol* for all moneymaking activities. The bazaar offers many positive opportunities as well as many challenges.

The first positive aspect of a bazaar is that it provides fellowship. People come together and work. It is an excellent tool for assimilating new members into the church by giving them a role or task. There is a sense of accomplishment and purpose. For many people it is one of the most exciting and exhilarating aspects of church life. Indeed, for some, it is the only time they are involved. Some people who attend church only once or twice a year will participate for hours in preparation for the annual bazaar.

A related opportunity that the bazaar provides is the feeling of unity. When people are working toward a common goal, they are too preoccupied to be divisive. The work and the project, the activities and the deadline date, tend to provide an environment for teamwork that reflects unity within the Body of Christ. Many who have a need to belong, but do not fit on a board or committee or want to run for an office, can participate and find a sense of belonging.

Third, there is a sense of accomplishment. Many of the activities of the church are not easily measurable. When people attend a Bible class and grow in their Christian faith, they experience a part of the Christian life that is difficult to quantify. But it is easy to measure how many gallons of chili were made, how many quilts were sewn, how many place mats were assembled, and how many people ate hot dogs during the bazaar.

Another positive aspect of the bazaar is that it uses many of the talents and gifts of the members. Those who are involved have a sense of utilizing their gifts, pursuing their hobbies, investing their skills, under the general banner of "the work of the church" and for the benefit of others who will come and obtain the articles or eat the food.

A fifth opportunity that the bazaar offers is to invite the community into the church. Community people become more familiar with the building and meet people who are members of the church. This can sometimes lead to further contact with people and may help them to consider the church as their religious home.

The annual bazaar also provides some challenges. When the goal of the bazaar is overtly communicated or subconsciously intimated as a way of making money, it projects an image that the purpose of the church is to make money. Because the bazaar is so highly publicized and because the atmosphere of taking money in exchange for goods and services is so prominent, the message comes through loud and clear to the unchurched person who attends the bazaar.

Another challenge is that the money gained may lack a specific purpose. The bazaar will be of greater benefit with a specific purpose that is communicated very clearly and continuously among those who are involved and anyone who might attend.

It is of further benefit to make the purpose selfless. The church can choose to provide ministry beyond itself. This reflects the love of Christ to the community. The funds collected from the bazaar can provide help to a nonchurch family whose house burned down, to a nonchurched young person who has a serious illness and expensive medical bills, or to some other important ministry in the community.

A third significant challenge to the annual bazaar is to combat society's idea that "all the church wants is my money." The Christian church has received a large amount of adverse publicity. Highly visible Christian leaders have been exposed as having mixed motives for fund-raising. This provides an environment in which any money-raising activity involving nonmembers is particularly dangerous.

The annual bazaar with a money goal can also severely undermine the financial stewardship understanding of the people within the church. The biblical teaching of stewardship directs the Christian to give *from* what the Lord has given, not *to* a project (like a bazaar, or money given for a craft item or a piece of pie). While proper stewardship understanding can be communicated clearly, when money changes hands in response to a service or goods offered by the church, the issue of "giving from what the Lord has given" is easily lost.

Finally, does the annual bazaar represent good stewardship of time? Is the effort worth it? Is the money worth it? If 50 people are involved in a bazaar and it nets $2,000, and each person spends about 10 hours either serving at the bazaar or preparing for it, then that results in 500 people-hours. That equals a rate of $4.00 per hour. What would happen if the same people each donated $40.00 and spent 50 hours, instead, reaching out to unchurched neighbors and friends?

Here are six keys to provide a positive experience for the annual bazaar or any financial project in the church.

1. *Make it outreach-oriented.* Obtain names and addresses of people who participate from the outside. Design a follow-up mechanism to share the good news of Jesus Christ and invite them into the fellowship of His Church.

2. *Do it for others.* Hold the bazaar with an intention to serve others and not maintain the church.

3. *Enjoy the fellowship.* Since fellowship, unity, and camaraderie are by-products of the bazaar, encourage fellowship at every level of the activity.

4. *Downplay the money.* If money is part of the strategy, make it as minimal as possible, not just by amount, but also when communicating the project.

5. *Give yourself away to your neighbors.* Consider providing everything for free. If you want to share your talents and gifts with others, do it. If you want to share your good cooking with others, do it. One youth group demonstrated this when they had a free car wash for nonmembers only. While the kids washed the cars, the pastor and an elder introduced themselves to the drivers and invited them to church.

6. *Have a clear focus and goal.* Whatever the goal is, make sure that it is clear and well communicated to all those involved.

Financial Intricacies

The economy of the rural church is intricate and complicated. When Greg's grandfather farmed the family farm, he used a team of horses. Today, Greg rides in a combine with an electronic ignition and air-conditioned cab. He talks to his wife at the farmhouse through a two-way radio. In the southeast corner of the bedroom where his grandfather was born, Greg has a computer where he keeps the farm books and analyzes his earnings.

The rural way of life has many specific challenges and many wonderful opportunities for the rural church that will be sensitive to the unique life-style of agricultural people and what that means in the use of their money.

9

Design for Growth

*K*im had been canning vegetables since early morning when Char stopped by for a chat and a cup of coffee. Their conversation drifted around to the church. They had both been in the church a long time and had seen it go through many ups and downs. They recalled the years that Pastor Ulmer had led the church. He was energetic and exciting, but somehow the worship attendance didn't grow and the church wasn't involved in outreach.

Both remembered the days following Pastor Ulmer's leaving. The church was without a pastor for almost two years. Professors from the nearby seminary came, but it was always someone different. It seemed like they would never find another pastor.

Then Pastor Kulick came. Everyone was excited and enthused. It was great to have someone to call "Pastor" after two years. Pastor Kulick had troubles in some other churches, but the superintendent felt he could start over by coming to this church. Things were OK for a while but then began to deteriorate. Finally the church split, and Pastor Kulick took several families with him to start another church. That left the church pretty small.

Attendance had dwindled to an average of 40. Seminary professors came and filled in again, and students came and practiced, but there was a lot of discouragement among the people. Five pastors were called. Each refused. Perhaps it was the meager salary, or perhaps the recent history. The members had almost given up. But they were committed. For many, their grandparents had belonged to this church. So they hung on. They had known tough times before. These people were survivors through drought and blizzards and crops rotting in the field. They looked at their church life the same way.

Then three and a half years ago, Pastor Kelly had come. When he was interviewed, most thought he would never agree to come to such a small congregation. But Pastor Kelly was looking for a challenge, and his heart went out to these people. He loved their spirit as much as he recognized their need. He made it clear that he was committed to the growth of God's kingdom and that if they wanted to grow, he was their man. They called Pastor Kelly, and he became their pastor.

"Our church has really changed over the last few years," reflected Char.

"It sure has," agreed Kim.

"Do you think it's just because of Pastor Kelly that our church has grown so and that people are so excited about growing in their faith?" asked Char.

"I think that's part of it, but I think it's more than that. Pastor Kelly is gifted and works hard. But not everybody likes him. Some of the traditional people don't like all the changes he has brought to our church."

Char remarked, "We have had other good ministers. Remember Pastor Ulmer?"

"It's more than just the man," said Kim. "It's what he stands for. He is so committed to growth. He makes Bible study such a priority. It seems like he has sensitized all of us to want to look for people who are unchurched and help them to know about the Lord. You know, one of the things I noticed soon after Pastor Kelly came is that he began to talk about the purpose of the church. I had never really thought about that. All these years in the church and I don't remember anyone asking that question."

Char broke in, "You know what else? I never really thought about the church much in terms of outreach. I sort of felt it was for those of us who had been in it all these years. Somehow, I never applied to myself the Great Commission to go and make disciples. Now I don't see it that way at all. In fact, even if Pastor Kelly left next week, I don't think I'd look at the church the same ever again."

Purpose

The rural church is a wonderful place for ministry. It has

tremendous potential and great opportunities to reach people for Jesus Christ. Many of the people are strongly committed to the church and dedicated to their Christian faith. The rural church can be directed from being a self-centered, maintenance-oriented body to an outreach platform for reaching the community. There can be a design for growth.

One of the key ingredients for this design is to help the church recognize its purpose. What is the church there for? What has God called the church to do and to be? Why did Jesus die on the Cross? Why has He sent His disciples in mission? What did He mean when He said to go and make disciples of all people?

The experience that Char and Kim reflected was a reordering of their worldview concerning the purpose of the church. Pastor Kelly spent much of the first two years of his ministry sharing with the people a new vision for what the church ought to be. The people were receptive to this because they saw a great need for a pastor. The church had been without one for some time, and they were quite willing to follow the lead of a new person.

He spent a lot of time helping them look at Scripture. He conducted a Bible study called *Six Faces of the Christian Church*. It was a study that helped zero in on the images Scripture uses concerning the church. He related, through that Bible study, how the people of the church can see the church as God has intended it to be seen. Their understanding of what it means to be the people of God began to change. They began to reshape what church growth people call their philosophy of ministry.

Most of all, Pastor Kelly recognized that the key to the needed change was not a programmatic element. It was, instead, the worldview or perception of the people. An attitudinal change was necessary.

Leadership

Before developing an understanding of that attitudinal change, it is important to recognize the vital role of leadership. Pastor Kelly was a strong pastor and good leader. He understood rural culture. He was sensitive to the relational aspects of his leadership. He worked with the church, joined their history, and then worked to change it for the growth of God's kingdom.

Pastor Kelly's involvement in the Church Growth Movement helped shape his ministry and gave him the passion and the desire to increase the vision of the people in his new congregation. Pastor Kelly understood clearly the principles of church growth. He understood what it took to change people's attitudes. He was gentle but persistent. He loved the people, and he let them know it. But he was also strong in his leadership. His bias was that he was to be the leader and the congregation was to be equipped for ministry. This was a subtle but dramatic change in the style of leadership within the church.

Previously, the church had made the decisions and then told the pastor to go do the ministry. This meant that programs and priorities were often chosen by the whim of well-meaning but untrained laypeople. Then, the pastor—the one who had been trained in Bible college and seminary—was given the task of ministry.

Pastor Kelly had learned the biblical concept of leadership. He was committed to what the apostle Paul discusses in chapter 4 of Ephesians. He understood his role to be an equipper of God's people for the work of ministry. That meant that he was to help people identify their gifts and to equip them in their gifted areas so that they could do ministry in the ways God provided for them.

The people knew there was something different about Pastor Kelly right away. That first Sunday they had a potluck dinner. The president of the congregation, Dan Marth, asked the pastor to lead in the prayer. The pastor took Dan aside so that he wouldn't be embarrassed and said, "Dan, you can pray. You're a fine Christian man. You lead the church in prayer for this meal. I'm your pastor. I'm here to lead you, direct you, encourage you, inspire you, and teach you, but I'm not your hired prayer person. All Christians can pray. You're the leader of this congregation. You lead in prayer."

Dan was a little surprised but quickly thought of a compromise. He said, "Pastor, you pray this time. I promise I'll pray after this." That was the end of pastoral prayers at potlucks. It was also the beginning of Dan leading the group in prayer. It was the beginning of a style of leadership in which the pastor would direct, encourage, and lead the people to do the work of ministry. The prayer itself was not the real issue. It was only the symbol of a style of leadership in that church.

Pastor Kelly's style of leadership empowered the people and released them to do the work of ministry. Pastor Kelly not only added his energies to the work of the Kingdom at the church but multiplied them. This is a key principle of church growth, and it is the biblical way to reach the world for Jesus Christ. God's way is not addition but multiplication.

Not everybody liked this style of leadership. Pastor Kelly knew that with his church growth training he would automatically raise many people above their comfort levels. Some would respond positively. A few would rebel. He understood the risks and was willing to take them. His commitment was to the Lord and to these people. He recognized that an attitudinal change was the basis of everything that was to happen in that church.

The Development of Attitudinal Change

In Philippians 2, the apostle Paul says, "The attitude you should have is the one that Christ Jesus had" (v. 5, TEV). Attitude is our posture toward ourselves, our church, our community, and our world. Paul knew that sometimes we have to *see* things differently before we can *do* things differently.

Pastor Kelly understood that if the people were going to reach out to their neighbors, welcome visitors, provide visitors' parking, put up a sign at State Road 3 and County Road 12, remodel their building, build new bathrooms, restructure their worship to be visitor friendly, and make evangelism calls, it would first take an attitudinal change.

Without talking about how the people had to change their attitudes, thereby insulting or intimidating them, Pastor Kelly simply began to teach about the attitude of Christ from Philippians 2.

1. *Jesus was a servant.* He emptied himself. He humbled

himself before God. He was willing to come to the world and become one of us. He didn't have an attitude of superiority. He didn't say, like many churches say, "If they want to come, let them come. They know where we are."

2. *He was sent by the Father.* Jesus came into this world. The Father sent Him to us. He didn't expect us to go to Him. Likewise, the Christian Church is to go to people and be where they are.

3. *Jesus was obedient.* Jesus was obedient to the Father. He came to this earth to do God's will. He followed through. He was willing to pay the price so that people might be saved.

These things listed in Philippians 2 are not just what God theorized. They are what God did in Jesus Christ. They also represent the attitude of God in Jesus Christ. Pastor Kelly taught the church the importance of that attitudinal framework. He taught the people not only to do what Jesus did but also to be as Jesus was.

Pastor Kelly also recognized that real attitudinal change takes place not through a program but in a process. It usually takes multiple events to change people's attitudes, particularly if they have had those attitudes for many years.

Pastor Kelly understood this. He exposed the people of his church to church growth thinking through a number of different events. He understood that for the average person to experience attitudinal change and act upon it, seven significant exposures to the new thinking would be necessary. Over a slow, determined, challenging, and loving process, he began to expose his people to church growth thinking.

Pastor Kelly recognized two types of "roadblock people" in his church that frustrated the design God had for His kingdom. People who did not understand was one type. These were the people who needed to learn through Bible study, preaching, and other learning events. The other type of person was the apathetic person. Apathetic people need to be challenged before they will learn. They must become unhappy or frustrated before they will be willing to change. Pastor Kelly would need to be like an Old Testament prophet, challenging the people of God to see God's will. Once he raised the level of discontent among some people, there would be those who would turn against him, fight him, and seek his demise. He was clear about these repercussions of his important ministry. When they happened, he was not surprised.

Pastor Kelly recognized that in the process of attitudinal change, there are at least six *catalytic elements* that provide a boost of energy to jump-start a church stalled in the rut of maintenance and self-centeredness.

1. *The use of an outside expert.* Pastor Kelly slowly helped the church board see the value of having an expert consultant come into the church to measure its effectiveness and present recommendations.

The outside consultant sent questionnaires and surveys to the church prior to making an on-site visit. These were circulated among a random sampling of the congregation. Curiosity arose about why certain things were asked and what the results might be. The church received a long form to fill out asking for statistical information. The consultant asked the church to send a bulletin, newsletter, a budget, a copy of the constitution, and any brochures the church regularly used. These would be analyzed by the consultant.

Then the consultant came on-site. During his several-day visit, he interviewed people in half-hour segments from midmorning until late evening. He met with several of the boards and committees. He asked a lot of questions. Prior to his visit, anyone who wanted to interview with the consultant was asked to sign up. Three people did that and had their opportunity to be heard. The consultant promised that all the interviews were confidential. They felt that someone very important, an expert, was going to listen to what they had to say and would make a final report with numerous recommendations.

Several weeks later, the consultant returned to make an oral report to the congregation and to provide an opportunity for people to ask questions or comment about the report. Copies of the report were made, and anyone in the congregation could sign out a copy and read the entire report.

After the oral report, the congregation had 90 days to write an action plan for each recommendation. The action plans were sent to the consultant for approval.

It was a busy time after that consultation. The consultation raised the awareness of the congregation and brought excitement to the people. It served as a catalytic element bringing energy to the process of change that began to take place.

2. *The development of a philosophy of ministry.* As one of his primary recommendations, the consultant encouraged the congregation to develop a philosophy of ministry statement. This mission statement was to describe the uniqueness of the church and its purpose and focus. The church had never done that before. It was a marvelous opportunity to wrestle with what the church was, how it was unique, and what it could do in the future.

The step-by-step method, provided to develop the philosophy of ministry, was designed so that all the members could take ownership in the process. As Pastor Kelly noted, the process of developing the philosophy of ministry was just as important as the final statement itself.

The church used this philosophy of ministry in publicity to the community and in the preparation of a brochure that described the church. When new members came to the church, they received a brochure that clearly indicated what this church was all about.

3. *Analysis.* Another catalytic element for attitudinal change in the church was an analysis of the church and its community. Pastor Kelly led the people to develop a questionnaire in which, on a random sampling basis, they visited many of the people throughout their mission area. They asked people what the church could do to help them. They learned some key methods of meeting the needs of people in their area and finding bridges over which the gospel could travel.

They had never done this before in the church. It was an exhilarating experience for those who were involved. It was also exciting when those who were not involved heard the results of what had taken place through the survey.

4. *Cognitive and affective learning.* One of the things Pastor Kelly understood was that if their attitudes were going to be affected, the people had to be exposed to learning processes that were both cognitive and affective. The people needed head knowledge but also had to learn through experience. So, Pastor Kelly had many guest preachers and speakers come to share their testimonies of how God had moved their churches from a maintenance mode to a mission mode and how their church had grown.

Pastor Kelly also showed several films that were available for rental. He helped the people see other Christians who had wrestled with change, accepted it, and developed a new attitude toward growth.

Pastor Kelly recognized the importance of helping people capture the enthusiasm of new members who came into the church. He gave new members an opportunity to give testimony to the entire church. Many of the new members would mention how friendly the church was and how excited they were to know Jesus Christ. This motivated the people to want to share their faith even more.

As part of this affective training, Pastor Kelly led his people through a life-style evangelism program. He helped them share their story of faith with people who were their contacts. As they learned this particular evangelism program, they shared their faith in small groups in the congregation. This provided experience for the people. This, too, is a strong element in the process of change for growth.

5. *Modeling.* Pastor Kelly recognized the importance of modeling for the people of his church. Therefore, three Sundays a year he took key leaders to different churches. He always chose a church that was growing. They observed as much as they could and then had lunch afterward and debriefed. By the time the leaders had done this at the third church, they were beginning to be good at identifying special principles that were used in these growing churches.

Pastor Kelly warned the leaders not to borrow the programs of the growing churches. Instead, he said they should be architects themselves. They should take the general principles that were involved in the programs and ask how these principles could take shape in their own church. The more they did this, the more the leaders became expert architects of Christian principles for church growth.

6. *Self-fulfilling prophecy.* Pastor Kelly was clearly committed to change in a positive way. He recognized that people are motivated not by the law but by the gospel. He understood the biblical truth that we must be obedient to the Great Commission. But while that is a truth, it is not a good motivational tool. A better motivational tool is to help people recognize that by God's grace they are free from guilt and sin. Out of God's love and mercy, they have been given the privilege of being ambassadors for Jesus Christ in this world.

Recognizing this positive method of motivation, Pastor Kelly provided self-fulfilling prophecies for the congregation. He didn't tell them they ought to be friendly to visitors. Instead, in front of them, he would tell visitors how friendly the church was. He would not make people feel guilty because they did not go to Bible class. He simply emphasized how thrilled he was that many people in the church saw the value of studying God's Word.

As the people in the church heard these expectations from their pastor, many of them responded and rose to the expectation level of their leader.

Not everyone responded with a change of attitude, however. How many responded? About 20 percent of the core membership. While this might be discouraging to many pastors, Pastor Kelly understood the 80-20 rule that applies to any organization, including the church. The 80-20 rule goes like this: 20 percent of the people do 80 percent of the work. Twenty percent of the people give 80 percent of the money. This is true of the human family at any time in history in any culture. Twenty percent of the people lead and shape the future, and 80 percent of the people follow along.

Pastor Kelly knew that once an attitudinal change took place among 20 percent, the church would actually do a turnaround and begin to change. Following the 80-20 rule, Pastor

Kelly intentionally spent 80 percent of his time cultivating, directing, equipping and training this 20 percent of the people—and the church grew!

Ways to Grow

In every rural setting there are two ways in which a church can grow. Every church can grow up and every church can grow together. Every church can experience growth in the grace and knowledge of Jesus Christ. Members can grow in their discipleship walk. Further, people can grow together in unity and harmony. Koinonia, the cement that is provided by the New Testament power of God's love, can grow stronger. This can happen in any rural church, even if the numbers of people in the area are dwindling. Every church can grow up and together.

Some churches can also grow out. There are rural churches located in vast communities where many people do not know Jesus Christ. They might say they belong to a church, but they are *functionally* unchurched. Rural churches can reach these people because rural churches are filled with members who know these people. Once rural church people have an outreach attitude and are equipped through a life-style evangelism program, many rural churches can grow out.

Furthermore, many rural churches can grow more. This is the growth that comes by starting new churches. One of the easiest ways a rural church can grow is by planting a church within a church. This takes place by starting a new worship service at another time, preferably in a different style of worship. Within many rural areas, there is the need for an alternative style of worship that will communicate better to a different kind of people found in that area.

Additionally, there are areas where other churches can be planted. Church planting is one of the fastest ways God's kingdom grows. Many churches have the opportunity to start a new work in a neighboring town or community.

Harvest Urgency

When it is time to harvest, it is time to harvest. There is no time to get a haircut. There is little time for social activities. If a hydraulic hose breaks, it needs to be repaired *now*. If the truck that is needed to haul grain has a flat tire, the tire needs to be repaired *now*.

People in agriculture are people who understand the urgency of the harvest. Everyone knows that harvesttime doesn't last forever. The right conditions for harvest don't continue very long. Harvesttime comes and goes quickly.

Jesus said, "Take a look at the fields; the crops are now ripe and ready to be harvested!" (John 4:35, TEV). He was not talking about grain. He was talking about people. Today there are many people who need to be reached for Jesus Christ. There are billions worldwide. Many millions live in rural areas that are within the ministry of rural churches. These churches, once moved by an attitudinal change, can be a powerful force for the work of Jesus Christ in the lives of these people. People in the agricultural setting know how to work hard, and they know how to work fast when they have to. They understand the harvest. God can use them as a mighty force for building His kingdom.

Selected Bibliography

Barber, Diane, and Kent Hunter. *Facing the Facts for Church Growth*. Corunna, Ind.: Church Growth Center, 1982.

Board of Parish Services, Lutheran Church—Missouri Synod. Pamphlet, *Hope for a Time of Crisis: Facing Challenges in the Agricultural Community*. St. Louis: Concordia Publishing House, 1986.

Byers, David M., and Bernard Quinn. *New Directions for the Rural Church*. New York: Paulist Press, 1978.

Dudley, Carl S. *Making the Small Church Effective*. Nashville: Abingdon, 1978.

Hassinger, Edward W., John S. Holick, and J. Kenneth Benson. *The Rural Church: Learning from Three Decades of Change*. Nashville: Abingdon Press, 1988.

Hunter, Kent R. *Foundations for Church Growth*. New Haven, Mo.: Leader Publishing Co., 1983.

———. *Moving the Church into Action*. St. Louis: Concordia Publishing House, 1989.

———. *Six Faces of the Christian Church: How to Light a Fire in a Lukewarm Church*. Corunna, Ind.: Church Growth Analysis and Learning Center, 1983.

———. *Your Church Has Doors: How to Open the Front and Close the Back*. Corunna, Ind.: Church Growth Analysis and Learning Center, 1982.

———. *Your Church Has Personality*. Nashville: Abingdon Press, 1985.

Madison, Paul O. *The Small Church: Valid, Vital, Victorious*. Valley Forge, Pa.: Judson Press, 1975.

McGavran, Donald A. *Understanding Church Growth*. 3rd ed. Grand Rapids: William B. Eerdmans Publishing Co., 1990.

Quinn, Bernard. *The Small Rural Parish*. New York: Parish Project, 1980.

Richardson, John. *Ten Rural Churches*. Great Britain: Federation for Rural Evangelism, British Church Growth Association, and Church Pastoral Aid Society, 1988.

Schaller, Lyle E. *The Change Agent*. Nashville: Abingdon Press, 1972.

———. *Growing Plans*. Nashville: Abingdon Press, 1983.

———. *It's a Different World*. Nashville: Abingdon Press, 1987.

Smith, Rockwell C. *Rural Ministry and the Changing Community*. Nashville: Abingdon, 1971.

Sullivan, Bill M. *Ten Steps to Breaking the 200 Barrier*. Kansas City: Beacon Hill Press of Kansas City, 1988.

Surrey, Peter J. *The Small Town Church*. Nashville: Abingdon, 1981.

Wagner, C. Peter. *Leading Your Church to Growth: The Secret of Pastor/People Partnership in Dynamic Church Growth*. Ventura, Calif.: Regal Books, 1984.

———. *Your Church Can Grow: Seven Vital Signs of a Healthy Church*. Glendale, Calif.: Regal Books, 1976.

Wagner, Stephen A. *Heart to Heart: Sharing Christ with a Friend*. Corunna, Ind.: Church Growth Center, 1985.

Walrath, Douglas Alan. *New Possibilities for Small Churches*. New York: Pilgrim Press, 1983.

Willimon, William H. *Preaching and Worship in the Small Church*. Nashville: Abingdon, 1980.